THE LIBRARY OF HOLOCAUST TESTIMONIES

In the Shadow of Destruction

The Library of Holocaust Testimonies

Editors: Antony Polonsky, Sir Martin Gilbert CBE, Aubrey Newman, Raphael F. Scharf, Ben Helfgott MBE

Under the auspices of the Yad Vashem Committee of the Board of Deputies of British Jews and the Centre for Holocaust Studies, University of Leicester

To Forgive ... but not Forget by Maja Abramowitch
An End to Childhood by Miriam Akavia
My Own Vineyard by Miriam Akavia
From Thessaloniki to Auschwitz and Back by Erika Myriam Kounio Amariglio
Scorched by Irit Amiel
A Village Named Dowgalishok by Avraham Aviel
In Hiding by Benno Benninga
Journey through Darkness by Willy Berler
A Child Alone by Martha Blend
A Little House on Mount Carmel by Alexandre Blumstein
Like Leaves in the Wind by Rita Blattberg Blumstein
My Heart in a Suitcase by Anne L. Fox
Have You Seen My Little Sister? by Janina Fischler-Martinho
Good Beyond Evil by Eva Gossman
My Private War by Jacob Gerstenfeld-Maltiel
No Place to Run by David Gilbert
An Englishman in Auschwitz by Leon Greenman
Who Are You, Mr Grymek? by Natan Gross
Nešarim by Thelma Gruenbaum
A Life Sentence of Memories by Issy Hahn
Life Strictly Forbidden by Antoni Marianowicz
The Children Accuse by Maria Hochberg-Mariańska and Noe Grüss
With a Yellow Star and a Red Cross by Arnold Mostowicz
For Love of Life by Leah Iglinsky-Goodman
From the Edge of the World by Anne Joseph
Hasag-Leipzig Slave Labour Camp for Women by Felicja Karay
Out of the Ghetto by Jack Klajman with Ed Klajman
A Cat Called Adolf by Trude Levi
Wartime Experiences in Lithuania by Rivka Lozansky Bogomolnaya
Fire without Smoke by Florian Mayevski (with Spencer Bright)
Hiding in the Open by Zenon Neumark
The Jews of Poznań by Zbigniew Pakula
My Child is Back by Ursula Pawel
From Dachau to Dunkirk by Fred Pelican
From Berlin to England and Back by Peter Prager
My Lost World by Sara Rosen
From Lwów to Parma by Klara Rosenfeld
Warning and Hope by William Samelson
Fortuna's Children by Paul and Imre Schonberger
Surviving the Nazis, Exile and Siberia by Edith Sekules
By a Twist of History by Mietek Sieradzki
Through Blood and Tears by Henry Skorr
Memoirs from Occupied Warsaw by Helena Szereszewska
I Was No. 20832 at Auschwitz by Eva Tichauer
I Light a Candle by Gena Turgel with Veronica Groocock
Lessons in Fear by Henryk Vogler
Trust and Deceit by Gerta Vrbová
The Girl in the Check Coat by Christine Winecki
Holocaust in the Ukraine by Boris Zabarko

In the Shadow of Destruction

Recollections of Transnistria and Illegal Immigration to Eretz Israel, 1941–1947

YOSEF GOVRIN

VALLENTINE MITCHELL
LONDON • CHICAGO, IL

First published in 2007 in by Vallentine Mitchell

Catalyst House, 720 Centennial Court
Centennial Park, Elstree, WD6 3SY

814 N. Franklin Street
Chicago, IL 60610

www.vmbooks.com

Translated from the Hebrew original, *Be-Tzel ha-Avadon*, published by Beit Lohamei Haghetaot Press 1999, in collaboration with Yad Vashem, Jerusalem, and the Centre of Research of Romanian Jewry, the Hebrew University of Jerusalem

British Library Cataloguing in Publication Data

Govrin, Yosef
In the shadow of destruction : recollections of
Transnistria and illegal immigration to Eretz-Israel,
1941–1947. – (The library of Holocaust testimonies)
1. Govrin, Yosef – Childhood and youth 2. Jewish children
in the Holocaust – Ukraine – Transnistria (Territory under
German and Romanian occupation, 1941–1944) – Biography
3. Holocaust, Jewish (1939–1945) – Personal narratives
4. Jews – Persecutions – Ukraine – Transnistria (Territory
under German and Romanian occupation, 1941–1944) 5. World
war, 1939–1945 – Personal narratives, Jewish
I. Title
940.5′318′092

ISBN 978 0 85303 643 2
ISSN 1363 3759

Library of Congress Cataloging-in-Publication Data

A catalog record has been applied for

Printed and bound by CPI Group (UK) Ltd, Croydon, CR0 4YY

Contents

List of Illustrations

To my children
and grandchildren

The Library of Holocaust Testimonies

Ten years have passed since Frank Cass launched his Library of Holocaust Testimonies. It was greatly to his credit that this was done, and even more remarkable that it has continued and flourished. The memoirs of each survivor throw new light and cast new perspectives on the fate of the Jews of Europe during the Holocaust. No voice is too small or humble to be heard, no story so familiar that it fails to tell the reader something new, something hitherto unnoticed, something previously unknown.

Each new memoir adds to our knowledge not only of the Holocaust, but also of many aspects of the human condition that are universal and timeless: the power of evil and the courage of the oppressed; the cruelty of the bystanders and the heroism of those who sought to help, despite the risks; the part played by family and community; the question of who knew what and when; the responsibility of the wider world for the destructive behaviour of tyrants and their henchmen.

Fifty memoirs are already in print in the Library of Holocaust Testimonies, and several more are being published each year. In this way anyone interested in the Holocaust will be able to draw upon a rich seam of eyewitness accounts. They can also use another Vallentine Mitchell publication, the multi-volume *Holocaust Memoir Digest*, edited by Esther Goldberg, to explore the contents of survivor memoirs in a way that makes them particularly accessible to teachers and students alike.

Sir Martin Gilbert
London, April 2005

Introduction

I was 10 years old when Nazi Germany and Fascist Romania launched a surprise attack on the Soviet Union on 22 June 1941, all along their common border. By the beginning of July 1941 their armies occupied the provinces of Bessarabia and Northern Bucovina, where I was living with my parents and the other members of our family.

One year earlier, on 28 June 1940, these provinces had been cut off from Romania and annexed to the Soviet Union – following an ultimatum presented by the Soviet government to the Romanian government to vacate these provinces within 48 hours. Romania had no choice but to give in. The alternative would have been to oppose the Soviet Union by force, which at that time Romania was unprepared to do alone.

The Soviet ultimatum to Romania – without its knowledge – was based on a secret memorandum of understanding between Germany and the Soviet Union on the partition of 'areas of influence' attached to the 'Mutual Non-Aggression Pact' signed in Moscow on 23 August 1939 by Foreign Ministers Ribbentrop (Germany) and Molotov (Soviet Union) – better known as the Ribbentrop–Molotov Agreement.[1]

I was 13 when, on 20 March 1944, the soldiers of the Red Army liberated the Moghilev Ghetto in Transnistria – an area in southwest Ukraine, between the Dniester and the Bug rivers – placed under the Romanian Occupying Administration according to a memorandum of understanding signed between Nazi Germany and Fascist Romania in August 1941 (known as the Tighina Agreement).

We were brutally transported to Transnistria in autumn

1941, shortly after the Romanian forces had massacred tens of thousands of Jews in Bessarabia and Northern Bucovina,[2] at the order of the Fascist leader of Romania, Ion Antonescu. Along with the survivors of the massacres deported to Transnistria were the Jews of South Bucovina and the Dorohoi districts – integral parts of Romanian territory. The Jews of these two districts, like the surviving Jews of Bessarabia and Northern Bucovina, were also deported to the ghettos and extermination camps of Transnistria while the invading armies of Germany and Romania advanced deep into the territory of the Soviet Union.

During these death marches to Transnistria my father was killed, and many members of our family – who had lived in Edinitz and its surroundings – perished. The total number of Jews who died during the Holocaust of the Jews of Bessarabia and Bucovina is estimated at about 300,000. Only 50,000 Jews remained alive on the day of liberation in March 1944 out of the 120,000 Jews who had been deported by the Romanian authorities to Transnistria. My mother, two of her sisters, and I, miraculously, were counted among the survivors.

I was 16 when together with my mother I reached the shores of Eretz Israel (then Palestine under British Mandate) as illegal immigrants. We sailed on a cargo vessel, the *Knesset Israel*, carrying 3,800 illegal immigrants. When we reached the port of Haifa we were stormed by sailors of the British Royal Navy who forced us – after a hand-to-hand battle – to abandon the vessel and transfer to three British destroyers that carried us to the British detention camps in Cyprus.

After eleven months of detention in the Cyprus camps (by that time I was nearly 17) we were permitted – this time legally – to immigrate to Eretz Israel within the framework of the 750 *aliyah* (immigration) permits granted monthly by the British Authorities to the Cyprus camps inmates. (The number of permits monthly totalled 1,500, with the other 750 going to Jewish refugees displaced in Europe, mainly in Germany.) It was October 1947, about six weeks before the UN General Assembly decided on the partition of Palestine into two states,

Jewish and Arab. The British authorities held us an additional two months in the immigrant detention camp in Atlit near Haifa behind barbed wire, under strict military surveillance. In December 1947 we were released unconditionally, once again becoming free people.

The strong compulsion to be absorbed into Israeli society, in all its domains of activities, in the shortest period of time, the striving to complete my secondary school studies – while working for my living at the same time – and later on the long years of my academic studies (for my BA, MA, and PhD) and the many tasks I had to carry out during my 42 years in the diplomatic service of the State of Israel, all of this somehow pushed aside, consciously or unconsciously, my recollections of that terrifying period of my life in the shadow of death in Transnistria – pushed aside but not forgotten.

The oral evidence I gave during January–February 1993 in a video interview to the Department of Evidences of the Yad Vashem Memorial Institute in Jerusalem constituted the basis for these chapters of my recollections. They are described here from the point of view of a child and an adolescent, a survivor of this Holocaust, as they were engraved in my memory. Here and there they are depicted against the historic background of my parents' home and the town of Edinitz, where I spent my childhood before the outbreak of the German–Soviet war. A concise chapter of these recollections was published in *Yalkut Moreshet* in November 1997.

In this book I have broadened the scope of events and added a new chapter on my illegal immigration to Eretz Israel, which lasted a bit more than a year.

Let this testimony serve as a memorial candle to the Holocaust victims of Bessarabia and Bucovina and to all the rest of the victims of the Holocaust who, much to our deep sorrow, did not survive to see the Victory Day over Nazi Germany nor the rebirth of the State of Israel.

Yosef Govrin
Jerusalem, 2007

1 My Childhood Surroundings: Edinitz and My Parents' Home

I was born during the week of the Festival of Hanukkah in December 1930, in Czernowitz, the capital of Bucovina, to my mother Fradia (later Zadcanit), *neé* Lerner, and my father David Gurvitz. When I was still quite young, my parents and I moved to Edinitz, a townlet in Bessarabia.

Both of these provinces – Bucovina and Bessarabia – had been annexed to Romania in 1918, after the end of the First World War. Twenty-two years later, the Soviet Union took control of Bessarabia and North Bucovina following a Soviet ultimatum to Romania, on 26 June 1940. Reluctantly, Romania was compelled to accept it, without a fight but with profound bitterness, so deep it had a decisive influence on events as they developed in the region. Several months later Romania was compelled to relinquish North Transylvania (which it had annexed from Hungary in 1918) to Hungary and South Dobrogea (which it had annexed from Bulgaria in 1918) to Bulgaria. The Romanian nationalist parties put great pressure on King Carol II to abdicate for having given his acceptance to these territorial concessions without a struggle. In fact, he was impeached and went into exile.

His son, Crown Prince Mihai, took over the throne from his father, but the real power was usurped by the nationalist-fascist dictator, Marshal Ion Antonescu, who ruled Romania from September 1940 until his arrest in the Royal Palace on 23 August 1944 in complete collaboration of King Mihai, who declared an anti-fascist revolt, thereby joining the Allied Forces in the final stage of their war against Nazi Germany.

Shortly after becoming Romania's dictator, Ion Antonescu made an alliance with Adolf Hitler, Germany's Nazi dictator, and on 22 June 1941 under his rule, Romania joined Germany in the surprise attack on the Soviet Union. Antonescu's aim was, among other things, to regain the lost provinces – namely, Bessarabia and Northern Bucovina – that the Soviet Union had forcibly wrested from Romania a year earlier and to reintegrate them into its territory.

As early as the first stage of the German–Romanian attack on the Soviet Union, at the beginning of July 1941, the invading armies conquered these two provinces. For Antonescu, however, this was not enough, and Romania continued to fight alongside Germany against the Soviet Union until the anti-fascist revolt in August 1944, when the Soviet Union's army, advancing toward the west, edged closer and closer to Romania's eastern border. In the course of the Soviet counter-attack the Red Army liberated Bessarabia and Northern Bucovina at the end of March 1944, and once again they became an integral part of the Soviet Union.

With the dismantling of the 15 Soviet republics in 1991, Bessarabia became an independent state called Moldova (under Soviet rule it had been the Moldavian Soviet Republic), while North Bucovina – annexed under Soviet rule to the Ukrainian Socialist Republic – continued to be part of the independent Ukraine.

Although we lived in Edinitz, our roots were firmly in Czernowitz. Every year we visited it. Apart from the fact that members of our family to whom we were very close lived there, my mother was particularly attached to this city. After completing public school (eight grades at that time) in her native Zabriceni, a village in the vicinity of Edinitz, she relocated to the university city, Czernowitz, to continue her studies. There she graduated with distinction from the Hebrew Seminar for Teachers and Kindergarten Teachers, founded by the countrywide Federation of Hebrew Schools and the Safa Ivria (Hebrew-language) organization. This was the only institution of its kind in Romania for preparing educators to teach Hebrew and Jewish studies.[3]

Upon completion of the programme at the Hebrew Teachers

Seminar, the graduates were sent to the various Jewish communities that had Hebrew schools and kindergartens. My mother was assigned to teach in Berhomet, Falticeni, Oradea, and Dorna. As part of her studies in Czernowitz and her pedagogical work in Bucovina, my mother had learned the German language and culture. She was also involved in student activities and became acquainted, for the first time, with Zionist leaders and Jewish personalities who deeply impressed her with their speeches. These figures included visitors from abroad drawn to Czernowitz because of the wide range of Zionist and Jewish activities concentrated there. My mother brought a great deal of this spirit with her to Edinitz.

Czernowitz was only 120 km (75 miles) from Edinitz, but during my childhood years there was a large cultural gap between them expressed in different standards of living and quality of life. I well remember that every time I travelled from Edinitz to Czernowitz, I felt as if I was moving along the timeline of progress that separated them. For me Czernowitz was the gate to a magnificent, enlightened world that would light the torch of imagination for any child growing up in a provincial town such as Edinitz, then underdeveloped in comparison to the Viennese lifestyle of Czernowitz.

About two years after my parents' marriage, and with me in tow, they moved to Edinitz. Our home soon became a focal point for Zionist and public activity as well as a meeting place for the local intelligentsia, emissaries from Eretz Israel, and representatives of Zionist and public organizations.

My parents were active members in Po'alei Zion (a socialist-Zionist ideological party), and my mother also belonged to WIZO (Women's International Zionist Organization). She was, however, mainly engaged in teaching Hebrew and Jewish studies to young people, especially to *halutzim* (pioneers) who intended to make *aliyah* (immigrate) to Eretz Israel.

From the little I remember of my father and from the meagre information I have about him, he was a modest, dignified man, quick-minded, intelligent, and always ready to help anyone in need.

My father was born at the beginning of the twentieth century in a small village, Badragi, in the vicinity of Edinitz; all the local Jews were engaged in petty trade and agriculture. Fewer than ten Jewish families lived there; there was no Jewish school or permanent synagogue. On Saturdays and holidays, the home of my grandparents, Yosef and Sossia Hurvitz, served as a house of prayer. They passed away before I was born.

From an early age my father was engaged in marketing agricultural products to the big cities and in importing consumer goods and clothing to his shop in the village. During the First World War he was mobilized into the Tzarist army and served somewhere in Russia. Released at the end of the war, he returned to his family and his previous occupation in his native village that had been transferred – as was all of Bessarabia – from Russia to Romania. Later on he bought some land for agriculture, specializing in the cultivation of grains for exportation. His occupation often brought him to the large Romanian cities, where he became acquainted with the urban way of life.

His Jewish and secular knowledge he acquired through private teachers from the surrounding cities brought to his parents' home, where the family's seven children were growing up. He supplemented his studies as an autodidact by reading books and learning foreign languages, gaining a fairly good knowledge of them, including Hebrew – which became the language of the house in our home in Edinitz. Studying Torah (Mosaic law) and Jewish lore was his main interest. Attracted by the Jewish national revival movement, he dreamt – together with my mother – of making *aliyah* to Eretz Israel.

His firm faith in the God of Israel graced him with the spiritual stamina and self-confidence needed to overcome the difficulties and hindrances he encountered during his truncated lifespan. I am quite sure that even on the death march that put an end to his life, his lips were whispering a desperate prayer to the creator of the world.

My father's love and devotion to his family knew no bounds. For him our warm home was a creative nest where he found tranquillity and spiritual inspiration in his daily struggle to make a living – a living constantly threatened by endemic anti-Semitism, a by-product of the anti-Jewish policy of the Romanian governments, particularly after Bessarabia's annexation to Romania.

To the little ones, and to me in particular, he was a teacher and a friend. To the adults he was a father and a faithful brother in joy as well as sorrow. He had many plans for our family when the thread of his life was suddenly snapped by the nefarious murders, and he was only 41 years old.

Looking back to that period, our house in Edinitz seems to me to have been a combination of a religious-traditional way of life and a liberal-national one. The Sabbath, the holidays, and *kashrut* were strictly kept. Although my father prayed morning and evening, he did not wear a *kippah* (skullcap) while conducting his daily affairs. On holidays I used to accompany him to the synagogue where the majority of worshipers belonged to Zionist organizations. Many of them were frequent visitors to our home.

My parents subscribed to the Yiddish daily *Unser Zeit* (Our Times), published in Kishinev, and to other magazines in Yiddish and Hebrew, produced in other cities. This meant they could follow events in the Jewish world, in our region and in Eretz Israel, sharing their information and views with their visitors. Moreover, they read these publications in addition to the Romanian newspapers published in Bucharest that reached Edinitz after some delay.

What did the discussions in our house focus on? Anti-Semitism and its manifestations in Romania and the rest of Europe, Jewish settlement in Eretz Israel, possibilities for *aliyah* and emigration, Zionist activities, newly published books of specific interest – all these dominated the exchange of ideas among us.

We had no radio (I doubt that anyone in Edinitz had one). We did, however, own many books in several languages: German literature that my mother had brought from Czernowitz; Russian literature that my father had collected during his bachelor years; books in Yiddish and in Hebrew, including the traditional Jewish religious works.

In our living room hung framed pictures of Sir Moses Montefiore, Ahad Ha-Am, Eliezer Ben-Yehuda, Perez Smolenskin, Haim Nahman Bialik, and others. It looked like a gallery of personalities, with each figure expressing his personal contribution to contemporary Jewish and Zionist history. Alongside these was a certificate issued by the Keren Kayemet l'Israel (the Jewish National Fund) attesting to the planting of ten trees in the Herzl Forest in Eretz Israel – a present from my grandparents (on my mother's side), Yehoshua and Lea Lerner, to my parents on the occasion of their marriage in Elul (September) 1929. Adding to all that the fact that Hebrew was my mother tongue, I would not be mistaken in noting that, in comparison to other homes in Edinitz, ours was probably unique in its national spirit.

On Jewish holidays our house was suffused with a holy spirit. The Passover preparations were the most demanding that I remember. My mother put in long, hard days in readying the house. The matzot were ordered well in advance from a local Jewish bakery and kept in a big wooden crate in an isolated room. On the eve of Passover, all the special plates and cutlery were taken down from the attic, where they were stored all year long – except for the Passover week – so that no *hametz* (leavened food not kosher for Passover) could reach them, God forbid. At the end of the holiday, they went right back into storage. My father used to lead the reading of the Haggadah using tunes he had learned from his father, Yosef Halevi Hurvitz, who had heard them from his father and grandfathers. On Shavuot (Pentecost) our rooms were decorated with green branches and leaves and white flowers, wafting their delicate scents all over the house. On the eve of this holiday, my schoolmates and I would walk to our homes, with flower wreaths crowning our heads. All along as we made our way we would sing '*Saleinu al keteifeinu, rasheinu aturim, miktzot ha-aretz banu, heveynu bikkurim*' ('Our baskets are on our shoulders, our heads are decorated; we have come from the corners of our Land, we have brought first fruits'). This favourite song we had learned in kindergarten, as it was and still is sung in Israel, for the Shavuot holiday.

Thanks to my parents I was brought up in a national-traditional spirit, with the Hebrew that was dominant in our home (in addition to Yiddish) being my mother tongue, a unique phenomenon in our town in those days.

The source of this influence was my grandfather (my mother's father), Yehoshua Lerner, a rabbi and *shohet* (ritual slaughterer), a widely learned man and an ardent Zionist, who served the Jewish population of the surrounding villages. He taught all his ten children (seven survived the First World War) Hebrew and Judaism, educated them in the Zionist spirit, and encouraged them to leave for the big cities (first Odessa, and after the First World War, Czernowitz) to attend institutions of learning and thus broaden their knowledge while acquiring culture. All seven of his children graduated from the Hebrew Teachers Seminar in Czernowitz, following which they taught Hebrew and spread the Zionist idea among the Jewish communities where they worked – in Romania, South America, detention camps in Cyprus, and Israel.[4]

My grandfather, together with my grandmother Lea Lerner, cultivated a meeting place for the local and surrounding intelligentsia in their rural home in Zabriceni. Here literary debates were held with the participation of youth from the entire area. Their home was also the site for Zionist activities for settling in Eretz Israel. The intellectual stimulation created in their house was a unique phenomenon in the Jewish way of life in a Bessarabian village.[5]

All this took place before my parents brought me to the world. By my childhood years, the 1930s, the majority of the younger generation of Zabriceni had already spread all over the world, to America, Eretz Israel, the big cities of Bessarabia and Bucovina, and elsewhere seeking ways for self-realization, whether as *halutzim* or members of the free or other professions: medicine, science, law, literature, teaching, and journalism.

At the end of the 1930s few of the young people remained in the village. The soldiers of the fascist Romanian army, who invaded it in early July 1941, organized – with the collaboration of local Christian villagers – the mass killing of the thirty families living there. Only eight persons escaped death, and after a few weeks they were deported to the ghettos and death camps of Transnistria; only four of them survived and returned to Zabriceni after its liberation by the Red Army.[6]

Many remembered my grandfather's illustrious role in the ideological fermentation that so characterized the young adults in the village and its environs. I, who did not live in this village but knew it as a child from our visits to my grandparents, always admired him very much because of his great educational, cultural, and ideological influence on shaping the nature of the young generation.

Edinitz, at that time, retained its small town character, typical of the Bessarabian landscape: small shops, petty trade, agricultural cultivation using the old-fashioned methods, minor industry for producing soap and oil. No paved roads – the whole town covered in swampy mud: in spring, after the melting of snow; in autumn, with the beginning of the heavy rains. Freezing winters. Heating by burning sunflower hulls or, in the best case, wood in primitive stoves built into the walls of rooms. Outhouses. No telephones in the houses, no running water, no drainage canals, limited electricity used only in the evenings, no public transportation, no permanent movie house, no theatre (except for a performance or two annually by a wandering Jewish theatre group). A very modest hospital and one pharmacy (both Jewish-owned). Two to three physicians (Jewish), two to three lawyers (also Jewish).

Before the war (1941) Edinitz had about 8,000 inhabitants, of whom some 80 per cent were Jewish, the remainder being Moldovians, Russians, and Ukrainians.[7]

The spoken language among the Jews of the town and those living around it – as in all other Jewish communities in Bessarabia – was Yiddish. A minority, and this included the intellectuals, spoke Russian and Hebrew. With the Christian residents, with whom there were daily business contacts, they spoke Moldavian (originally Romanian) and Russian-Ukrainian. As a rule there were no social contacts between the Jewish and non-Jewish population. The Jews regarded themselves as strangers in an alien surrounding, with spiritual and moral values superior to those of the non-Jewish inhabitants. This explains why no signs of assimilation appeared among the Jewish population in local society. The Jewish community, in general, was united, preserving its religious-traditional way of life. The majority had a national-liberal orientation that found expression in Zionist education and in *hakhshara* ('training') towards *aliyah*, in the study of Hebrew, and in the nurturing of a Jewish-Zionist library called Tarbut ('culture').

We avidly followed the events in Eretz Israel, the progress in settling its land, and especially, the tragic events of Arab terror and violence in the period 1936–39. Many of our acquaintances were worried about the well-being of their sons and daughters, who were among the founders of the kibbutzim Avuka, Masada, Hulda, and Hanita and who, as members of these kibbutzim, were often engaged in repelling the Arab attacks against them (particularly in Hanita). Other youth groups in our town were advancing through the training stages and were about to join kibbutzim. Among those who joined kibbutz Yagur were my aunt, Sonia Lerner,[8] and Liova Gucovski (later Yehuda Ahisar),[9] who parachuted into Romania in October 1943, was captured and imprisoned, and was then freed after the anti-fascist revolt in Romania on 23 August 1944.

Dozens of *halutzim* made *aliyah* to Eretz Israel in those years. Many others were preparing through their *hakhshara* for *aliyah*.[10] In many instances those on the verge of *aliyah* took lessons in Hebrew and language literature from my mother, so that our house, too, was in a certain way involved in the fate of those who emigrated to Eretz Israel, founding new settlements or joining existing ones.

From time to time local representatives of Keren Kayemet and Keren Hayesod came to Edinitz from various parts of

Bessarabia and Bucovina to collect money for the resettlement of Eretz Israel, be it by draining swamps, planting trees, or expanding agriculture and irrigation. I do not remember emissaries from Eretz Israel stopping in Edinitz, but it did happen that former residents who had moved to Eretz Israel and settled in towns or cooperative settlements came back for short visits. Many members of the local Jewish community who intended to make *aliyah* would meet with the 'visitors from Eretz Israel' to find out about the economic, political, and security situation there and about possibilities for absorption. I used to accompany my parents to such meetings and I remember the questions and answers continuing until well after midnight. In those days, these visitors carried out an important task by disseminating relevant information about Eretz Israel.

Edinitz was also a spiritual, religious, and economic centre for the Jews living in the neighbouring villages and their environs. It had a warm Jewish community in which everyone knew one another and was interested in each other's welfare. Should anyone pass away, the tidings would immediately be spread throughout the town and hundreds would attend the funeral, even people who had not known the deceased personally. The same was true of the weddings celebrated in our town.

The thin layer of intellectuals had limited influence on others. They comprised mainly self-taught teachers well acquainted with Yiddish, Hebrew, and Russian literature, who often led discussions on literary subjects and on current affairs. The majority of the community, however, was far from eastern and western culture, being deeply involved in the daily struggle to insure their survival – a battle that took up much of their time; only the Sabbaths and holidays were entirely devoted to prayer and rest.

Beside the Zionist activity that seemed to provide the main content of ideological life, a minority among the younger generation were communist activists who believed, as did many others in different places, that the solution to the 'Jewish question' lay in an egalitarian society forged in the spirit of

Marxist theory. I do not remember any ideological dispute between them and the Zionists. Although the communists were a small minority, acting clandestinely, the Romanian authorities took the phenomenon as sufficient to prompt manifestations of hatred against the Jewish community as a whole, since communist activity was strictly forbidden.

Many members of the Jewish community, including my parents, belonged to Zionist organizations that ran the gamut from left to right. Numerous young people were involved with the pioneering movements, on their way to *hachshara* and then to Eretz Israel. I, too, as a child belonged to Gordonia (a socialist-Zionist movement). My parents enrolled me in it since the movement's ideology corresponded with their Zionist approach. I was the youngest in this group and was quite happy to be counted among the grown-ups preparing themselves for *aliyah.* My dream for when I would be an adult was to make *aliyah* together with the those *halutzim* to settle in Eretz Israel.

The communal organization in our town included cultural and welfare institutions: a hospital, *moshav zekenim* (home for the aged), public schools (through fourth grade) where the Bible and Hebrew were taught in addition to the required subjects taught in Romanian state schools, and religious schools (Talmud Torah) where only the Holy Scriptures were taught.

My parents registered me in a private Jewish school owned and run by a learned intellectual teacher, Hirsh Kuzminer.[11] After having completed the fourth grade in his school, in summer 1940, I was supposed to be sent to a *gymnasium* (secondary school) in Czernowitz. At that time Edinitz had no *gymnasium*, quite surprising for a town with thousands of Jewish residents. A private *gymnasium* had been established in the 1920s, but it was closed down in 1936 following an order issued by the Romanian authorities. I do not know the reason why. But since other secondary schools were closed elsewhere in Bessarabia at that time, one may presume that the authorities acted out of political motives rather than pedagogical reasons. The majority of *gymnasium* teachers had been Christians, while the majority of students had been Jewish. After 1936 any pupil who wanted to continue secondary-level studies therefore had to travel to faraway cities where such schools still existed or, alternatively, remain at home and study privately for a few years and then take what was called an 'external examination' in a big city. For each of these scenarios a great deal of money was needed to cover the expenses (and not every Jewish family could afford it), and a large amount of ambition on the part of the student was needed to excel in his/her studies. Since the examiners were all Romanians aiming to hinder the Jewish pupils, we were obliged to know our material much better than any non-Jewish pupil. Even then, the director of the Jewish elementary school had to bribe the Romanian examiners – and such was the case in my school, too – to insure beyond any doubt the award of the desired certificate verifying that we had passed the exams.

I remember the times preceding the Soviet annexation (June 1940) of Bessarabia and North Bucovina as a period of insecurity – social, economical, and personal. The Romanian governments, which were frequently replaced, conducted at the close of the 1930s an openly anti-Semitic policy. The worst of those governments was the Goga-Cuza one that ruled for a relatively short period, from December 1937 to February 1938, but which had time enough to frighten the Jews of Romania in general and the Jews of Bessarabia and Bucovina in particular. It published many anti-Semitic regulations to exclude the Jews from the fields of trade, industry, pharmacy, medicine, administration, and law. To restrict Jewish presence in those fields, the Goga-Cuza government passed a law making it necessary to prove Romanian citizenship. Jews had to prove they had been born in Romania with birth certificates, which many lacked despite their parents and grandparents having been born where they were still living. The government conducted an anti-Semitic campaign in the Romanian press, which made many Jews fear for the future. The economic situation worsened and sources of livelihood were unavailable – all of this against the background of continuous confrontation between local Jews and the authorities in a poisonous, anti-Semitic atmosphere.

As a result many Jews, including my parents, sought a way to emigrate either to Eretz Israel or to America (North or South), but neither target was obtainable. My parents applied to various addresses but, unfortunately, were rebuffed by all. Looking back after the war, it seemed to me that had my parents – and many others, too – applied to the consular representatives of South American countries they might have obtained those much desired entry visas. Also, I am afraid they did not fully exhaust all possibilities for making *aliyah*. No guidance of any kind came for Eretz Israel. It is difficult, or even prohibited, to judge the past through the eyes of the present, but at that time it seemed to my parents and our relatives that there was no way out.

Under such circumstances it should come as no surprise that the annexation of Bessarabia and North Bucovina to the Soviet Union in June 1940 was perceived as actual deliverance, particularly in light of what we had heard from eyewitnesses and had read in newspapers about what was happening among the Jewish communities of Poland after its occupation by Nazi Germany. We and the others who frequented our home saw our rescue as a likely to fend off the threat of war. We also hoped that the anti-Semitic laws would be rescinded, so that we would be eligible for free education and health services and the chances for finding employment would be better.

For many in our area – and myself among them – the sight of the Soviet tanks approaching our town symbolized, as it were, an invincible force projecting a great deal of security. This prompted many members of the Jewish community to go out to welcome the Red Army soldiers joyously with flowers in hand. Even I, at 9 years of age, was there to applaud their arrival.

Later, we heard about alleged cases of local Jews humiliating Romanian soldiers retreating from Bessarabia and North Bucovina. Even if these claims were true, they did not characterize the behaviour of the general Jewish population in those regions. The rumours, however, were exploited a year later when the Romanian and German soldiers invaded these areas in their blitzkrieg on the Soviet Union. They served as the excuse for murdering tens of thousands of Bessarabian and North Bucovina Jews in revenge for the so-called degradation the previous year of Romanian soldiers by the Jewish population. The mass murders within a few days of the occupation of these areas were accompanied by horrible acts of mass rape of Jewish women and plunder of Jewish houses in close collaboration with the local non-Jewish population. The latter took this to be a fitting opportunity to strike out against Jews, drawing on their traditional hatred of them that had only grown during the Soviet regime (1940–41), when a number of Jews had carried out central tasks in the Soviet administration. This fact alone was sufficient for the non-Jews to identify all local Jews as assisting the Soviet authorities in establishing themselves within that period of time, much to the discontent of the local Christian population.

True, the Soviet authorities were assisted to a great extent by the local Jews. First of all, Jewish intellectuals outnumbered by far the non-Jewish. Secondly, the Jews were considered by the Soviets as more loyal to its regime than the non-Jews in view of two facts: the Jewish population under Romania's administration was persecuted by the anti-Semitic legislation and policy towards them; and the number of communist members among the Jews was higher than among the non-Jews.

The Soviet authorities began to plot to harass the Jews, whether because they considered them a rich group (an unfounded generalization), many of whose members' property was nationalized as early as the initial stage of the Soviet rule, or because they belonged to the Zionist movement (a true fact).

In either case our home was vulnerable. To be sure, my

mother was soon integrated in the educational network as a teacher in the Jewish state school founded in Edinitz (for grades one to ten, following the Soviet system), whose language of instruction was Yiddish, but the mere fact that she had belonged to a Zionist movement and been active in it was, now, not to her advantage. The land my father owned, although not extensive, was nationalized. As a result he could not continue with his previous occupation and had to seek other jobs, which he disliked. Moreover, he was considered a *kulak* (a property owner who had gotten rich by 'exploiting others'). Although Saturday was part of the workweek under the Soviet administration, my father, unlike my mother, was unwilling to take a job obliging him to work on the Sabbath – forbidden by Jewish law – since he strictly maintained the holiness of the day.

Because of these two 'sins,' Zionist activity and belonging to the class of landed property owners (even though we were by no means rich), my parents were afraid they would be put on the 'black list.' Their fear increased when on 13 June 1941 the Soviet authorities deported to Siberia many Jews – former Zionists and people considered to be rich – practically empty-handed. Among the deportees was my uncle (my father's brother) Meir Hurvitz, his wife Feige, and their two daughters, Sara and Ethel.[12] Included in the transport to Siberia were also a limited number of non-Jews considered Romanian nationalists or simply wealthy. Had the war not broken out, we can assume that the Soviet authorities would have continued to deport Jews from this area, and we might have been included.

Soviet machinations against the Jews appeared not only on the personal level but were actually expressed, on the whole, at the public level. Within a few months after the Soviet annexation of Bessarabia and North Bucovina, all Jewish organizations of a national nature just collapsed. The first to go were the Zionist parties along with the *hachshara* centres that had prepared the pioneers for their anticipated *aliyah* to Eretz Israel, and in their wake, all the Jewish community institutions that had existed for generations. The entire community leadership fell into disarray. From then on, both individuals and the ethnic community depended entirely on the city council. Since Jewish communal organization had been of typical solely of the Jews, it was now the Jewish population that was the chief – if not the only – victim of its dissolution.

Synagogues were the only institutions that continued to function as before, although attendance of worshipers on Sabbaths and holidays was rather limited since anyone with a government job had to work.

The Jewish education system, including the *hadarim* (religious schools), was forced to cease operation with the establishment of the state schools, which taught in three languages – Russian, Moldavian, and Yiddish – at which attendance was obligatory. Even though each of the schools served its own ethnic population, they were all characterized by Stalin's well-known saying about the education of national minorities: 'They should be national in form and socialist in content.' In practice that meant that among the subjects in the Jewish school curriculum none had any national Jewish character and, of course, the pupils had to attend the Jewish school on Sabbaths and holidays just like on any other school day (Sunday being the day off). The purpose of this policy was to detach the pupils from the Jewish roots they had been linked to since the day they were born. To be sure, this approach applied to the other schools as well, whether teaching was in Russian or Moldavian, but it was less disruptive for the pupils since their schools had been closed in any event on Sunday. So, again it turned out that we, the Jewish students, were the main victims of the system.

For me, as for the rest of my schoolmates, the transition to the Soviet educational system was relatively easy. During the year of Soviet rule I was in the fourth grade. (The Soviet authorities forced all pupils to go back to the grade they had been in under Romanian rule.) The teaching material was adapted to the Soviet curriculum and taught in Yiddish, including subjects we were learning for the first time: Yiddish language, stories from Yiddish literature, Russian language and literature, and the history of the Russian people. I was in high 'patriotic' spirits, since I found myself in a Jewish environment with the counselors organizing us – the 10-year-olds – to become pioneers (the preparatory stage before becoming *komsomols*), teaching us pioneer behaviour and patriotic songs in Yiddish and Russian. The song I loved to sing the most, with great enthusiasm and sincere belief, was the one my schoolmates and I sang for the May Day 1941 festivities, nearly two months before the outbreak of the war. Here is a free translation of its words:

> If a war broke out tomorrow,
> If a dark force should attack us,
> And we would have to march to the front,
> The entire Soviet people as one man
> Would rise to defend its free homeland …
> On land, in the air, and on the sea our song
> would ring out mightily and thunderously.
> If a war broke out tomorrow,
> I would be ready today for the march …

How much patriotic pathos resided in this song, and how much naiveté and confidence in the ability to defeat 'the dark force attacking us' (whose identity was left anonymous)! I was not the only one who identified himself so closely with this song. After the war it became clear to me that millions of Soviet people had shared that feeling with me, and, most importantly, that they were completely unprepared for any sudden German attack on the Soviet Union. I found reference to this in Soviet historiography that claims, among other things, the following:

> On the eve of the war much damage had been caused by the assumption that any enemy that would attack the Soviet Union would be defeated easily. Popular films, such as *Should a War Break Out Tomorrow*, repeatedly

> stressed this notion. Even some of the military newspapers adopted this line. Many writers and propagandists preached the dangerous idea that any fascist or imperialist country that would attack Russia would soon collapse, since their workers would revolt against their governments. They totally belittled the scope of the bedazzlement of the masses in the fascist countries; they made little of the value of fear as a deterrent factor operating on potential participants in uprisings and made light of the effectiveness of the promises made to soldiers, officers, and their families about the portion they would receive from the spoils of war.[13]

While the first part of this reference explains the psychological reason for which the Soviet Union was unprepared for a German attack on its territory, perhaps it is the second part that may explain the military reason for which the Soviet Union was unprepared for an onslaught against it: it relied too heavily on masses of workers in the fascist countries being unwilling to take part in such an attack in expression of solidarity between the proletarians of the world. To this one must add Stalin's blind confidence in Hitler, firmly believing that Nazi Germany would not strike the Soviet Union, since it had signed a non-aggression pact on 23 August 1939. He paid no heed, therefore, to the warnings from various political, military, and intelligence sources citing the exact date of the coming German attack on the Soviet Union.

Beyond that, I still well remember the official announcement in the press made by TASS (Telegraphic Agency of the Soviet Union) on 14 June 1941, in which the Soviet government dismissed fears of an approaching attack by German on the Soviet Union, denying rumours of German military concentrations along the western borders of the Soviet Union. This statement filled us with optimism, since we then could have had no inkling of its fictitious nature.

1. My parents' wedding day, September 1929. Top row (left to right): my aunt Sonia Lerner; my mother's cousin, Finkel Lerner; my uncle Yosef Lerner; my aunt Atara Lerner-Silbermann; my grandfather's niece, Esther Lerner; my grandfather's brother, Yehuda (Idel) Lerner; my aunt Nechama (Netty) Lerner. Middle row (left to right): my grandmother Lea Lerner; my mother, Zadcanit (Fradia) Lerner; my father, David Hurvitz; my grandfather Yehoshua Lerner. Bottom row (left to right): my aunt Batia Lerner; my cousin Leibele Bronfman; my aunt Shoshana Lerner.

2. My parents, Zadcanit (Fradia) née Lerner and David Hurvitz, Edinitz, 1929

3. With my parents, aged three, Edinitz, 1934

4. I am four years old, Czernowitz, 1935

2 *Outbreak of War: German–Romanian Blitzkrieg Against the Soviet Union*

The day the war broke out, 22 June 1941, found my mother and me in Czernowitz (Chernovtsy). On 17 June we had left our home in Edinitz, together with my grandmother Lea for a visit – scheduled as a short one – to my uncle and aunt, Yosef and Hanna Lerner. The main reason for our trip was my mother's wish for me to have me examined by a physician in Czernowitz, following a severe bout of acute pneumonia that had downed me in late spring that year so seriously that I barely survived. For a few days I had been delirious from the high fever that left my parents in a terrible state of shock. My illness was so serious that a rumour spread that I had already left this world. I remember my father standing near my bed with tears in his eyes, praying day and night for my recovery. When I finally defeated the disease my parents decided that I should be seen by a doctor in Czernowitz, since medical standards there were much higher than in Edinitz. The morning after our arrival in Czernowitz I already benefited from medical treatment I could not have found in Edinitz.

After the fact, I can say that this visit was crucial in our lives – the outbreak of war only a few days after our arrival immediately separated us – in Czernowitz – from my father in Edinitz. When we had said good-bye to each other 'for just a few days', we certainly had no idea that we would never meet again. Thinking about it today, I can still see the sadness on my father's face as my mother and I set out for Czernowitz. I will never know what he was thinking and feeling when we parted with *'Shalom, u-le-hitra'ot'*, but the bleak look he gave us as we left him at home has stayed with me all my life.

From the start of the war we were completely cut off from each other. In addition to the absence of any telephone connection, the strict prohibition against civilian movement along the roads near the front line meant we could not return to Edinitz, and my father, we assumed, could not travel to Czernowitz. Both cities – like all of Bessarabia and Northern Bucovina – were very close to the front line.

About a fortnight after the war had erupted, the German and Romanian armies had already occupied most parts of Bessarabia, including Edinitz, and the entire territory of North Bucovina, including Czernowitz.

During the mass murder of Jews in Edinitz, carried out by the Romanian soldiers as soon as they entered the town – with the assistance of local Christian residents who led the murderers to the Jewish houses – my father stayed hidden. The killing of the local Jews lasted three days (from 4 to 7 July 1941). About a thousand Edinitz Jews were brutally slain,[14] among them our neighbours from across the street, the Rosenberg family: Leibesh, Jacob, his wife Sarah, and their 10-year-old son Reuven – or Rivele, as we called him – who was my best childhood friend at play and at school from first grade until the bitter end in the fourth.

Leibesh Rosenberg had been a wealthy tradesman, so the Soviet authorities during their rule of 1940–41 nationalized his house and property, leaving him with nothing. He and his wife Tuba moved into his brother Jacob's place. I remember how embittered he was under the Soviets, when he more than once spoke, in the presence of my parents, in favour of the Germans, whom he saw in his imagination as more humanitarian and cultured than the Soviets. In the end, he was murdered during the first days of the German–Romanian conquest, together with the other members of the Rosenberg family except for his wife Tuba, who had been visiting her daughter and son-in-law in Czernowitz, a happenstance that saved her from certain horrible death.

While the killing was going on in the Rosenberg house, my good friend Rivele took shelter by hiding himself under a table covered by a long tablecloth. When the murders subsided, the local Christian mob started to loot the homes of the slain Jews, among them the Rosenberg house. While snatching the covering from the table, they discovered Rivele in his hiding place. They killed him on the spot, just as he was seated, and it was in that position that he was collected with all the other victims, so we were told, and taken to the mass burial site in the Jewish cemetery for eternal rest.

Hundreds of women and girls were taken to a nearby forest by the Romanian soldiers, who brutally raped them there. Only a few survived, and some of them committed suicide. Among them was my 10-year-old schoolmate Blimale Mutzelmacher, her two sisters, Esther and Zahava, and their mother Sima, all of whom had been raped in the presence of their father and husband, David, in their own home. After the rape the mother and her three daughters committed suicide by hanging themselves, and the husband/father threw himself into a well close to their home. I still remember the constant smile on Blimale's beautiful, young face. Even Satan himself would not have thought that this would be her bitter end.

After the liberation, survivors told us that in some instances a number of men from the Edinitz Jewish community had put up fierce resistance to the raping soldiers. Among them was my teacher and school principal, Hirsh Kuzminer, who organized a group of local Jewish men to defend their families and protect the honour of 40 women who were hiding in a cellar in fear of being brutalized. Thanks to the men's courageousness the Romanian soldiers' entry to the cellar was barred. For their brave act, every member of the group was executed.[15]

When the three days of killing and looting were over, the victims were collected on wagons and taken to the Edinitz Jewish cemetery for burial in three mass graves. We were also told that all those who helped with the burial were murdered when their task was done. Similar mass killings took place in all the Jewish localities of Bessarabia and North Bucovina. This was just the 'introduction' to the Holocaust for this Jewry. Less than two weeks later began the deportation of all surviving Jews from Edinitz and its surroundings. They were concentrated into two convoys and sent off in two directions.

My father and some of our relatives[16] were in the one that headed toward Ataki on the bank of the Dniester River and from there to Moghilev on the opposite side. When my mother, my two aunts, and I reached Moghilev two months later with a convoy of deportees from Czernowitz, people from Edinitz who had managed to escape from the convoy my father was in as it passed Moghilev told us what my father went through.

The information we received from the escapees from the Edinitz convoy as well as from other eyewitnesses we came across on our deportation route praised him highly – he rushed to help the elderly and the sick and the children in the convoy, all the helpless ones who were usually the first victims among the deportees. With his last drop of strength he assisted them, keeping the embers of the flickering flame of their lives burning for a bit longer. Our informants also described him as introverted, speaking little, and showing great concern for our fate, since he knew nothing about what had happened to us, was well aware of the massacres perpetrated by Romanian soldiers in every Jewish locality they entered, and daily witnessed suffering and terrible losses.

From Moghilev my father's convoy was deported to Scazinetz and from there southward to Yampol and back across to the other bank of the Dniester river, to Bessarabia, in unbearable heat, without water or food, totally exhausted. While interned in the Vertujeni camp – one of the cruellest stations along the death march to Transnistria – he was taken, along with other men, to an unknown destination by Romanian soldiers. One rumour had it that this group was taken to work and, ultimately, all were killed. According to another version, these men were taken to the Cosauti forest, where all were murdered. One thing is clear: none of them returned alive. To this day their fate is uncertain, and we do not know where my father found his eternal resting place.

My father was one of tens of thousands of Jewish men, women, and children whose lives were abruptly ended by Romanian murderers, even before Nazi Germany's decision on the 'final solution of the Jews' at the Wannsee Conference.

The Romanian soldiers and their local Christian collaborators treated the Jews like beasts, whether on the first day of their invasion to Bessarabia and North Bucovina in early July 1941 or whether in the ways they forced deportation on the survivors of the massacres two weeks later.[17] They mercilessly slaughtered any of the deportees who, owing to lack of food and water in the hellishly hot weather or to physical or spiritual exhaustion from diseases that erupted, could not continue the death march to Transnistria. The local Christian population – particularly the Moldavians – worked enthusiastically alongside the killers in robbing and looting in the towns and among the trekking deportees.

When I grew up and looked back on that period, I often asked myself about what I had been told of the brutality of the local Christians, and I tried to fathom the source of their deep hatred of the Jews. After all, the majority of Bessarabian Jews, particularly those living in villages and small towns, lived a miserable life from one day to the next. They struggled constantly to secure a modest living for themselves and their families. For centuries they had lived side by side with the Christians, trading with them and doing them no harm. Even as they waged their ceaseless battle for existence, the Jews worked together with the non-Jews who also benefited. Their occupations were interwoven – if the Christians had not been able to sell their agricultural produce to the Jews, they would not have been able to buy the products the Jews offered. Moreover, the Christians needed the Jewish craftsmen (tailors, blacksmiths, glaziers, metal workers, and so on), let alone the Jewish physician, who was often the only one available for miles around. Few local Jews were considered rich, ones who in terms of Marx might be seen as exploiters. These were the shopkeepers and owners of flourmills and soap factories, needed by Jews and non-Jews alike. Was this dependency responsible for the explosion of hate? For years I sought for any Bessarabian Christians who saved or even tried to save Jews from the massacres or deportation. I found none. Only recently did the Committee for Righteous among the Nations of Yad Vashem–Holocaust Martyrs' and Heroes' Remembrance Authority locate a number of such gentiles out of three million residents in Bessarabia on the eve of the German–Romanian invasion. In retrospect, it seems to me that the poisonous anti-Semitism burning in the hearts of the local Christians for many generations – owing to the preachings and teachings in their churches and environment – fit right in with the unbridled incitement against the Jews by several Romanian governments who ruled between the two world wars. That was followed by the integration of Jews into the Soviet hierarchy, hated by the Bessarabians, during the Soviet administration of Bessarabia 1940–41, which added fuel to the fire. Another aspect to consider is the anti-religious propaganda trumpeted by the Soviet authorities during that year; it hurt the Christians, perhaps even more than the Jews. In any event, since the non-Jews identified the Jews with the Soviet authorities' policy, and a relatively high percentage of Jews were members of the Communist Party, the gentiles saw the Jews as cooperating with the Soviets in spreading that propaganda – even though the Jewish population suffered from the propaganda no less, if not more than the Christians. This, too, probably worked to fan anti-Jewish hatred.

But the raging intensity of the venting of their anti-Jewish feeling probably stemmed from the intense encouragement the local Christians received from the Romanian soldiers – the liberators – who initiated the killing and the plundering. The soldiers had received their instructions in advance, two days before Nazi Germany and fascist Romania launched their surprise strike on the Soviet Union. The Romanian chief of staff ordered the commanders of all military units to kill Jews without mercy, since they were accused of espionage and of having attacked Romanian soldiers as they retreated a year earlier from Bessarabia and North Bucovina.[18]

The words of Mihai Antonescu, deputy prime minister of Romania and acting marshal (in the absence of Marshal Ion Antonescu, dictator of Romania), gave government authorization to this order. The message was contained in a statement he made on 3 July 1941 at a conference he initiated at the Ministry of the Interior in Bucharest and then distributed as a booklet entitled 'Instructions and Directives to the Administrative Inspectors and to the Deputy District Governors who are being sent to Bessarabia and Bucovina'. Paragraph 10 in the booklet deals with 'ethnic and political cleansing'. with Mihai Antonescu saying the following:

> We have now reached the most fitting historic moment for total ethnic liberation, for national revision, and for cleansing our nation of elements foreign to our [nation's] soul that have latched onto it like a parasitic growth to darken its future.
>
> To make sure we do not miss this fitting moment, we must be merciless. Let no one allow himself to be seduced by humanitarian philosophy that masks the interests of a most aggressive race … behind which we find a rapacious religion … The ethnic cleansing will be carried out by deportation or isolation of all Jews in labour camps from which they will no longer exert their nefarious influence, along with all others who are foreign to our lineage and whose behaviour is suspicious.
>
> To achieve ethnic cleansing the provincial governments will carry out the forced migration of Jews … who should be expelled beyond the border, since they have no reason to be in Bessarabia or Bucovina at the time that the national rights [of Romania] are being restored to these territories.[19]

About a week later these ideas were reiterated by the dictator Ion Antonescu, in greater detail, in his speech at the meeting of the Council of Ministers on 8 July 1941, where he said:

> I want you to be merciless. There is no room here for sweet humanitarianism … For fear that I shall not be properly understood among some of you who are still traditionalists: I stand for forced deportation of all Jewish elements of Bessarabia and Bucovina, who should be expelled beyond the border. I am also in favour of forced migration of Ukrainian elements, who have no reason to be here at this moment.
>
> I do not care if we are judged by history as barbarians … There has never been a moment in our history more auspicious (for carrying out my order). If it be necessary, you should use machine guns.[20]

These directives gave the Romanian occupying army the legitimation not only for killing Jews and expelling them with brutal force to the ghettos and death camps of Transnistria but also to 'mobilize' the cooperation of the local Christian population – among them elements that hated the Jews – 'to be merciless' in their assistance in murdering Jews and to humiliate to the core any survivors of the massacres and the death march to Transnistria.

Through their brutal acts thousands of Romanian soldiers and their commanders, as well as thousands of plunderers among the local Christians, completely lost their human image and all the human values on which they had been educated by their religious faith and their culture.

Marshal Ion Antonescu and his deputy Mihai Antonescu were executed in May 1946 in Bucharest after being sentenced by a Romanian court trying war criminals, but the thousands of anonymous soldiers who committed viciously cruel acts were never brought to justice. I fervently hope that their deeds will be remembered in eternal ignominy.

5. On the death march of the Jews of Bessarabia to Transnistria, Bessarabia, summer 1941. Photo from M. Carp, *Transnistria*. The first person in the third line from the left. without a shirt, appears to be my late father. Next to him, with a jacket in his hand, is probably his brother-in-law, the late Haim Grinberg. (Both of them were identified by myself and my cousin Buma Grinberg, Uncle Haim's son.)

3 Czernowitz, Romanian Occupation, Ghetto, and Deportation

Early morning 22 June 1941 – the day the war broke out – we were glued to the radio receiver. The voice of Molotov, foreign minister of the Soviet Union, announcing Germany's attack on the Soviet Union, sounded confused and hesitant. His concluding words, 'Victory will be ours', were seared into my memory (perhaps because they turned into a slogan during the war years), but they did reduce our fear and anxiety. We were shocked to hear of the German bombardment of Kiev and other cities in the western part of the Soviet Union. The drastic turnover from Germany as ally to the Soviet Union to aggressor with its unexpected attack was simply inconceivable. It became real for us only when the German air force began to bombard Czernowitz that same day.

At that time we were living in the apartment of my uncle Yosef and aunt Hanna Lerner, on the third (and top) floor of a large apartment building located on the main street (called Siebenbürgerstrasse under Austrian rule, until 1918, and Stefan cel Mare under Romanian rule). Today, in the Ukraine Republic, its name is Ulitsa Mira (the Street of Peace). All building tenants were Jewish except the maintenance man and his family.

Every time an alert was sounded we dashed to the ground floor. There were no guidelines on what to do in case of bombardment, and it seems to me that our family – like all the other Jewish families living in the building – responded more out of instinct than experience. Bombings became more frequent and the destruction grew. Our confusion and fear grew daily. General mobilization was announced. My uncle, Jacob Sinnreich, was among the first recruited and sent to a destination in the east, but we did not know where.

In the beginning of July 1941 the Red Army began its retreat from Czernowitz. Many of the young Jewish men who had not yet been called up went into the streets with knapsacks on their backs, aiming to join the Soviet Army as it withdrew. Heartrending scenes of departure and separation abounded. No one could judge if it was better to run away with the retreating soldiers or to stay in town. After the fact, we can definitely assume that scores, if not hundreds of Jewish families would have tried to escape eastwards before the German and Romanian troops entered the city had they known what was awaiting them.

Everything was so sudden. With the great confusion, total chaos reigned. On each of the two days before the Red Army's retreat, my mother waited in line all day to obtain a permit to travel to Edinitz. As fate would have it, when that sought-after permit was finally obtained, Edinitz was already under German and Romanian occupation. Undoubtedly those who issued that prized permit were unaware of that, or could not even conceive that the Red Army – which we all saw as invincible – would simply run away from the invading troops. In addition to the all-pervasive chaos, a great degree of demoralization had resulted from the shock of war, the unexpected retreat, and the profound fear of 'what's going to happen tomorrow'.

Members of our family, neighbours, and friends recalled the news they had read about what had happened to the Jews in Poland after the German army had invaded its territory, particularly Warsaw in September 1939. The flow of information about the fate of the Jews in the part of Poland occupied by the Germans ceased with the annexation of Bessarabia and North Bucovina, by the Soviet Union. The Soviet media did not report on happenings there, which explains how people received the impression – mistaken, of course – that things there were back to normal.

Many years later, in Israel, while investigating this issue at the academic level, I came to understand something that none of us had a inkling about at the time: that after the partition of Poland between Germany and the Soviet Union, the countries had signed an agreement according to which neither of the two would wage hostile propaganda against the other.[21] Thus the mystery was solved, explaining why Soviet media had concealed information about the horrendous Nazi acts against the Jews, deeds that we and everyone else among us remained ignorant about. Had we been aware of them, no doubt tens of thousands of Jews would have fled eastwards, not only from Bessarabia and North Bucovina but also from all the other territories on the brink of conquest by Nazi Germany during its unexpected attack on the Soviet Union.

By 5 July 1941 we were already under German–Romanian occupation. As early as the first days after their taking Czernowitz and its surroundings – as in all the other places their troops entered – they perpetrated a massacre of Jews. Immediately, the rumour about the killing and the plunder spread in every direction. Romanian soldiers regularly came to the apartment building where we lived and examined our documents, but they did not touch us. The tenants quickly discovered that if they put on the table a wristwatch, a gold ring, or any other item of value, the soldiers would go directly to the table and leave the apartment in peace. So it was that in each flat entered by the Romanian soldiers, there was a repeat performance of this 'show'.

We stayed at home, refraining from going into the streets, so it was only a few days later that we heard in detail about the killings of the Jews who had been executed in town. The number of victims was estimated at about two thousand, among them the chief rabbi of Czernowitz, Dr Abraham Mark, and other well-known members of the Jewish community.[22] We were deeply shocked and terribly frightened about what was going to happen to us. Shortly afterwards, Jews were ordered to wear the Star of David – the yellow patch – and restrict their movement in town to certain hours. Jews were barred from working in the free professions. Jewish physicians could treat only Jewish patients. Jewish pupils were prohibited from attending school – both private and state. Praying in the synagogues was forbidden, even on the High Holidays. Owners of radio receivers were ordered to turn them in to the Romanian authorities, on penalty of death to whoever would not comply. Hundreds of Jewish men were taken for forced labour.

This situation lasted for about three months, until the order was given to set up a ghetto in Czernowitz. During those months our life proceeded normally. We got used to all the prohibitions. At certain hours we were permitted to go to the market and buy food. I remember a few exceptional instances when Jews were taunted and attacked. If I sometimes lost my way in the streets of Czernowitz with my yellow badge on my shirt, I would go up to a German soldier for directions, but somehow not to a Romanian one. For some reason, I found the German's behaviour more cultured than that of his Romanian counterpart.

At that time none of us knew the dimensions of the annihilation. We saw the Romanian soldiers as crude and vulgar, their cruelty giving vent to their nature when they slaughtered Jews and looted their homes upon their entry into Czernowitz. The same applied to their issuing orders to wear the yellow patch or setting limits on Jews' movements in the streets, and imposing all the other prohibitions aimed at making the life of the Jews miserable. Since all the anti-Jewish orders were issued in the name of the Romanian governors, well known for their pernicious anti-Semitism, we took all our misfortunes as stemming from the Romanians rather than the Germans.

On 11 October 1941 the Romanian authorities published an order informing the Jews of Czernowitz of the establishment of a ghetto in town. Accordingly, all Jews were ordered to concentrate on that day by 6 pm within a defined area of Czernowitz. All those who had to abandon their homes were allowed to take with as much of their indispensable belongings as they could carry by themselves. The order did not say how long the Jewish population would stay in the ghetto, but a rumour spread among the Jews of Czernowitz of a possible deportation from the ghetto to Transnistria.

The area allotted for the ghetto was very limited. It encompassed a small quarter that had long been populated mainly by Jews. We were fortunate in that we had some acquaintances there – the Lehr couple, friends of my uncle and aunt. They lived on Wahgasse in a modest apartment. Since the building of my uncle and aunt, where we had been staying since our arrival from Edinitz, was not included in the area of the ghetto, we were forced to leave it the day the ghetto was proclaimed and move into the Lehrs' apartment, bringing with us only what we could carry in our hands and on our backs as we made our way along the streets. On top of this, some other refugees found shelter in the Lehrs' apartment. We were all crowded together on the floor.

The number of Jews living in greater Czernowitz before the war has been estimated at some 70,000,[23] but only a limited number had been residing in what became the ghetto. The number of Jews upon the establishment of the ghetto has been put at about 50,000.[24] The decline in Jewish population can be attributed to a number of causes: Soviet deportation (June 1941) of thousands of Jews to Siberia, mobilization of others into the Red Army soon after the outbreak of the war, and still others running away with the retreating Red Army. To these one must add the 2,000 victims killed in town by the Romanian soldiers in the first few days of their occupation of Czernowitz.

Each Jewish home in the ghetto was expected to take in Jews from the other parts of town outside the ghetto. Had we had to live in the ghetto for a long period, no doubt epidemics would have broken out owing to the crowded living conditions and insufficient sanitation. Chaos was rampant in the ghetto at that time, but above all loomed the fear of new decrees.

A few days after the ghetto was set up came the decree of

deportation to Transnistria. My mother and I took this with a bit of hope, since we assumed that we would meet up there with my father. Having heard that all the Jews of Bessarabia had already been deported to Transnistria, we naively thought we would be reunited with him. We were all extremely tense as the days in the ghetto passed before our banishment to Transnistria.

Soon enough we understood that the Romanian authorities were willing to grant residential permits in Czernowitz to rich people and to a limited number of physicians and engineers. The lucky ones who received such permits could return to their homes, while the remainder were destined for deportation to Transnistria. It so happened that my uncle[25] – in whose apartment we had stayed, as already mentioned, from our arrival in Czernowitz 'for a short visit' until expelled to the ghetto – was successful in obtaining such a permit for his mother, Lea Lerner, his wife Hanna, and their son Jacob,[26] in return for his mobilization to forced labour somewhere in Romania. For them it was a heaven-sent rescue, for us a sense of relief mixed with disappointment over not being included with them.

About 20,000 Jews received permission to remain in Czernowitz. We were told that this arrangement had been achieved through vigorous intervention by the mayor, Traian Popovici, arguing that these Jews were indispensable for ensuring the normal functioning of the city. His attempt to pressure the Romanian authorities to allow all Czernowitz Jews to remain met with resolute refusal. The situation of a mayor displaying such courage and bravery was a unique phenomenon. Thanks to him one-third of the Jews of Czernowitz were saved from deportation to Transnistria.

After the war Popovici left a heartfelt testimony of human and moral value, revealing his great struggle with the Romanian governors. First, he attempted to postpone the establishment of the ghetto, and when he could not avoid it, he invested great effort in obtaining permission to allow 20,000 Jews destined for deportation to Transnistria to remain in Czernowitz.[27]

But when Popovici was deposed as mayor of Czernowitz in June 1942, having been accused of sympathizing with the Jews and having issued residence permits to many of them, beyond the quota, the fate of nearly 4,000 Jews who had been allowed to stay changed dramatically. In June–July 1942 they were deported by the Romanian authorities across the Bug river in the Ukraine into a zone under the control of the German administration that bordered Transnistria on the west, which was under Romanian administration. Only after liberation (March–April 1944) did we learn from a small number of Jews who had escaped from there that almost all the 4,000 had been killed by German soldiers shortly after their arrival. There is no doubt that the Romanian authorities knew beforehand that this would be the deportees' fate.

Since my mother, her two sisters – Batia Sinnreich[28] and Shoshana Lerner[29] – and I were not considered 'indispensable' people, and since we did not have the necessary financial means to attain the desired permit to remain in Czernowitz, the four of us were destined for deportation to Transnistria.

THE DEPORTATION

Early on the morning of 17 October 1941, Romanian soldiers took us out of the ghetto area and led us towards the railway station. We covered the distance on foot, carrying – along with hundreds of other Jews – our meagre baggage, which at any rate didn't amount to much. At the station we were pushed into windowless cargo wagons that became sorely overcrowded. I could hardly find a breath of air, even as I pushed myself, as a child, toward the single narrow vent that allowed air into the sealed wagon, an opening located close to the roof. It seemed as if I would never reach that outlet.

Late in the evening the train stopped in an open, swampy area. We were ordered to leave the wagon and march towards the town Ataki on the Dniester. Across the river, on the Ukrainian side, we could see the lights of Moghilev, the first station in Transnistria, which was already under Romanian administration. The trek to Ataki was very long and hard and the more we marched, the more difficult it became since the ground was extremely swampy. Each step required great effort to pull one's feet out of the heavy, muddy bog.

Behaving brutally and beating us as if we were animals, Romanian soldiers constantly hastened us to take bigger steps. Those who could not keep up with the demanded speed tossed off part of their baggage to make their march easier. My mother and my aunts, seeing my difficult, slow steps, advised me to throw away my knapsack. I flatly refused and managed to hang on to it. In the end it turned out that we all benefited from my persistence. First, because my knapsack held all the belongings I had brought with me from Edinitz for our visit to Czernowitz – and they were not many. Second, hanging over my knapsack was a large bowl that, later on, became indispensable for us; we used it for washing ourselves and for doing the laundry, the little we had. This bowl helped us maintain our hygiene.

One of the soldiers hounding us to step quicker marched up to my mother and brutally pulled off her wedding ring from her finger. I remember my mother reacting in a way that seemed to me and to others around her to be useless. At the time I did not know how to appreciate it. My mother started to rebuke him in the presence of a younger soldier standing nearby. Her main thrust questioned: how did you all lose your humanity? Were you not born as human beings? Were you not brought up in a family, in human society? Look at how you are behaving, how can you do what you do, shoving women, old people, and children? What sin have they and all the others in this convoy committed? And what is this humiliating deportation for? When he replied to my mother very rudely, she said to him, 'You see, you're just proving what I've said to you.' The young soldier present at this exchange listened to her but did not react. The contrast between the rude reaction of a soldier who pulled off her ring and the soldier who listened but did nothing is etched in my memory.

I do not know if there were any similar instances of a conversation of this kind carried on between a persecutor and a persecuted Jew. Only later on, witnessing the barbaric acts of the Romanian soldiers, could I understand to what extent my mother had endangered herself by responding as an educator and teacher who still had faith in the high value of education.

With our last drop of strength we made it to the riverbank. Here hundreds of deportees from the convoy huddled together. There was great crowding, near-freezing weather and non-stop rain. The little food and water we had brought with us when leaving Czernowitz were almost gone. We waited in the mud. A rumour flashed that we were about to be transported across the river, to Moghilev on the other side.

And so it was. A few hours later we were ordered to set off on a primitive raft, woefully overcrowded with deportees. We heard that there had been cases of people falling into the river, either because of fatigue or as a result of being pushed by Romanian soldiers accompanying the convoy. Yet, truth be told, the primitive rafts themselves that sailed up and back could scarcely bear the weight forced upon them. I still wonder, even now, how it was that we did not drown in the river.

After we made it across the river, we were taken to broken-down barracks. Each of the hundreds of families set itself upon a small space on the floor. The first stop in Transnistria. What would tomorrow bring?

4 *Moghilev, Transnistria: Struggle for Life*

A chain of miracles happened to us from the day the German and Romanian soldiers occupied Czernowitz in July 1941 to the day we were liberated by the Red Army in Moghilev, March 1944. First, we were saved from the pogroms carried out by the Romanian soldiers against the Jews of Bessarabia and North Bucovina the day after they invaded these regions. Second, we were saved from being included in the first transport of deportees from Czernowitz to Transnistria. Those deportees experienced a long, tormented march – always on foot – crossing through townlets of Bessarabia, losing hundreds of them before reaching their first, but not their last, station, in Transnistria. The second transport of deportees, which included us, was dispatched directly from Czernowitz to Moghilev. For thousands of deportees Moghilev was the first station in a long, arduous trek inside Transnistria. For us Moghilev was the first and last station in Transnistria, from the moment we set foot there until the end of our deportation. We were challenged daily by the threat of annihilation while carrying on our struggle for life – at times a seemingly hopeless battle. In this, too, much to our amazement miracles occurred thanks to which we survived.

The morning after the crossing of the Dniester, Romanian soldiers began to take all the deportees out of the broken-down barracks, where we had been placed the previous night, to lead us to the main street and from there, in a long convoy, eastwards. No word was said about the destination.

While marching with the convoy we noticed a young boy walking on the pavement alongside us. He signalled to us to leave the group and to join him. To this day I remember the signal he made. It was as if I was enjoying my stroll down the middle of the street and someone called to me: 'Come on, walk with me on the pavement.'

My mother was the first to leave the line of marchers, crossing to the pavement. No soldier stopped her. Immediately, she signalled to the three of us to join her. So we, my two aunts and I separately moved towards the pavement, one by one. Our passage took seconds. Nobody stopped us. The young boy disappeared as if he had never been there. We found ourselves near a carpentry workshop. My mother opened its door and entered; the three of us trooped after her. Within seconds we were all inside. My mother asked the carpenter, in Russian, if we could take off our knapsacks and leave them in his shop. He showed no opposition to this idea. When the convoy was no longer in sight, we went out as passers-by, turning to side-streets without actually knowing where to go.

A lot of the homes had been destroyed. The soil was swamp-like. At a later stage we found out that the Dniester had overflowed its banks a short time before we reached Moghilev, flooding many parts of the town. Along our way we came to a closed red door to a small house. My mother knocked on the door and it was opened. We soon learned that a local Jewish family by the name of Kunis was living there. They looked at us and said, 'Come in.' So we did. They knew at once that we were refugees. As we talked with them we realized that the owner of the carpentry workshop where we had left our belongings was an acquaintance of the Kunis family. Towards evening, when we thought we would not be noticed, we went with Mrs Kunis to the workshop and found our knapsacks where we had left them. They contained our only worldly goods, modest property indispensable for our daily life.

The Kunis family took us in and kept us for several months, until the local Moghilev Jews were also deported eastwards and a ghetto was set up in a small part of the town for Jews deported from Bessarabia, Bucovina, and the Dorohoi district of Romania. Our friendship with the Kunis family also continued after their successful return to Moghilev from the death camp Peciora to which they had been sent. We in the ghetto tried to assist them in whatever way we could. We are still in touch with the family. (Two Kunis sons, Sioma and Busia, then children, now both physicians, emigrated as adults to Israel with their families, while the parents passed away in Moghilev 30 years after the war.)[30]

The convoy from which we had dropped out continued to march, as we learned afterwards, to the Scasinetz concentration camp, known to be one of the worst. After staying there a few weeks, the deportees were moved eastwards deeper into Transnistria – as always, on foot – leaving by the wayside many who had perished from hunger, exhaustion, thirst, freezing weather, or illness.

Although, while marching in the convoy through the streets of Moghilev, we had not noticed any others leaving it, we did learn later that many others had slipped out along the way. This stoked the anger of the Romanian governor of the town, who subsequently ordered the launch of a campaign to deport to Scazinetz any Jews who had left the convoy in Moghilev. As a result we had to wander from one hiding place to another, and more than once we hid in the cellar beneath the floor of the Kunis family home or in their small woodshed, while Romanian soldiers who were looking for us passed by, without noticing us.

The Romanian Gendarmerie succeeded in each such *aktzia* – and they were quite frequently launched – in tracing those deportees who had no permit to stay in Moghilev and then sending them on their way eastwards. This scenario repeated itself even after the ghetto was set up in Moghilev. The usual routine soon became familiar. The Romanian governor would announce the names of those destined for further deportation. After the Deportees Committee had been founded, the governor would apply to it demanding that it supply him with a certain quota of deportees for further deportation. I remember that in each instance the demand was to meet a quota of 2,000 people, sometimes even more, and if the quota was not met, he would send the Romanian Gendarmerie to search around deportees' dwellings. If they did not succeed in finding them, the Gendarmerie were ordered to kidnap deportees from the streets of the ghetto or to remove people from the hospital that had been founded in the ghetto by the deportees. These cruel acts condemned those hapless, penniless, kidnapped people – particularly those taken away from hospitals – to certain death. The kidnappings more than once caused tragic separation of family members, without those left behind in Moghilev even knowing about what had happened. This was particularly true of parents whose children had been taken.

Between one *aktzia* and another, we had to insure ourselves a minimum income. From time to time my mother and especially my aunts, Batia and Shoshana, would pick out an item from the belongings we had brought with us from our home and sell it in the local market to Ukrainian residents. Even that we had the opportunity to go out to the local market was in itself a kind of ray of salvation. Soon we realized, however, that this source of income was exhausted, since we had nothing left to sell, and that we would have to find other ways to insure our basic existence.

In addition to living in the incessant shadow of hunger and threatened sudden deportation, another great danger always lurking was infectious disease, which easily spread among the deportees, especially typhus. Beyond that, the physicians – who also suffered and died from it – had no medicines to give the ill, not even something to reduce high fevers. Sanitary conditions became particularly dangerous in the winter months of 1941–42, when typhus spread in the ghetto, felling thousands in its wake. I, too, caught typhus. Fortunately, I was the only one in our living space that came down with it. For a few days my fever was so high that I was unconscious. I ate practically nothing. The crisis of the disease usually occurred on the thirteenth day; those who made it through the crisis survived. Few were lucky enough, but I was one of them. When the disease had passed, I was totally exhausted. Several weeks went by before I could stand up and practise walking, taking small, slow steps. For a long time I lay in my bed wrapped up in myself, dreaming of a piece of fruit – a totally unattainable object – or of days past that I thought would never return.

We were six people sharing a tiny room. For five of us the problem was now how not to become infected with typhus. My mother and my aunts stayed next to me the whole time, devotedly caring for me. The fear that my five roommates would come down with the disease bore heavily upon me. As a child living among adults, I now felt that I had become a threatening factor to their well being with 'my' typhus. I was terribly concerned about what would happen if I infected them and they died because of me. From everywhere I heard about acquaintances who had come down with typhus, about some who had passed the crisis safely and others who had not been so fortunate. The general conclusion was terrifying, to hear how the death toll was rising from day to day.

Even more horrible was to move around in the streets in the mornings. Corpses were taken out of the houses and dumped on carriages. Rumours then rife put the number of daily dead at one hundred. This was the first time in my life that I saw almost naked dead bodies, piled one on top of the other in the wagons, being taken to the cemetery. I assume that their clothing had been removed immediately after catching typhus, since the belongings of the dead could serve the living, either to be worn or to be sold. Even when the death toll from typhus abated, the number of the dying did not decline, since many succumbed to other infectious diseases or to starvation. This meant that the terrifying scene of wagons collecting the dead continued almost the whole time we were in the Moghilev ghetto. The situation was alleviated a bit when the representatives of the ghetto deportees, assisted by the Jewish community of Romania, set up a local hospital that received a limited supply of medicines, which were never enough to meet all needs. Had it not been for the proximity to the Dniester river where the deportees could wash themselves and their belongings, particularly in the spring and summer, and thus maintain a certain level of personal hygiene, the death rate would probably have been even higher.

The transfer of the deportees to the ghetto several months after our arrival in Moghilev was relatively less dramatic than the move to the Czernowitz ghetto. Here we had nothing to lose. In any event, we had shifted from one hiding place to another. With the help of friends we found a tiny, dark kitchen in the new ghetto area and we settled in there. Twice, heavy stone pieces of the ceiling nearly collapsed on us during the night. Only thanks to my aunt Shoshana's waking us up on time did we manage to escape safely. This was a miracle. Had we been out only a few seconds later, all four of us would have been killed, because the weighty stones fell right on our beds. Afterwards we, and our neighbours, had to work hard to get those pieces of the ceiling out of our kitchen.

The feeling of kinship among the families (some had known each other previously for a long time) crowded together under one roof made the daily struggle for existence slightly more bearable. Three main problems faced us. First, vigilance – we had to remain constantly alert to avoid being caught and deported further eastwards. Second, basic existence – how could we make a living? The reservoir of our belongings was almost dried up. What would we do when there was nothing more to sell? And third, integration – how to become part of the daily life that had been organized in the ghetto?

The minute we heard that an *aktzia* was going to take place in the ghetto to fill the quota demanded for deportation, we rushed to hide ourselves, day or night. The Romanian Gendarmerie and the Jewish policemen used to go from house to house, checking deportees for permits to stay in Moghilev. Anyone who could prove they were equipped with such permits was exempt from the danger of further deportation. But a large part of the deportees had no such documents and were fated to be sent on unless they could slip away from the police. One time, we had ourselves locked in our kitchen and had the lock hanging on the outside door. When Jewish policemen came to search for us, they were told by one of the building's residents, Jacob Kornblitt[31] (who knew them well and who was actually keeping the key to the lock after shutting us up inside), that they should not wait for us, since we had gone away and not said when we would be coming back. All that time we waited highly tense and totally mute; we did not budge from our hiding place lest the policemen who waited a day and a night for our return spotted us when looking inside the small window. Seeing that we had not shown up, they decided to go leaving one policeman outside our door to stand for many more hours until our 'return'. Only after Kornblitt convinced him that it was a waste of time to wait for us did he leave. To the policeman's credit, I should say that he did not try to break in. The fact that he did not catch any movement inside or hear any whisper probably made Kornblitt's words even more effective, so he left after more than thirty hours of watching. We were safe again.

In the streets of the ghetto sudden inspections were taking place. People who were not eligible to stay in the ghetto were dragged off to the deportation convoy that would bring them to the concentration camps. The Jewish policemen who had been searching for us were armed only with sticks. If I had run away from them, they would have chased after me but could not have shot at me. It did happen that we were caught, together or even separately. Each time it happened we managed to escape from their grasp. So our lives went on, from one escape to another, from one evasion to the next.

Who was permitted to remain in the ghetto? In the first stage it was whoever could prove that he/she was a local Jew. So we obtained false documents for ourselves as local Jews. In the second stage, after the order to deport local Jews eastwards (we heard that some three thousand Jews were then living in Moghilev), we returned to our previous identity, with all the risks that involved. A considerable number of the deportees who remained in Moghilev acquired the necessary permit in exchange for paying a large amount of money to the Romanian governor. To those one should add the 'Turnatoria' Foundry workers and their families. At a certain stage our names were added to those one of the foundry's workers, an engineer by profession, and his family. This afforded us some protection, but we did not rely on it too much. Alertness, caution, sophistication, improvization, and, above all, good luck prevented our further deportation eastwards.

The 'Turnatoria', founded at the blessed initiative of a Jewish engineer, Siegfried Jagendorf, a deportee from Bucovina, was an outstanding enterprise, deserving all possible praises. Jagendorf succeeded in convincing the Romanian governor of the necessity for the foundry and its economic usefulness. Soon after its establishment the Turnatoria included workshops (carpentry, locksmith, and a garage for the repair of vehicles, tools, and equipment), employed about six hundred deportees and paid them a minimum salary, but the foundry's main importance was in getting permanent residence permits in the Moghilev ghetto for those workers and their families. Jagendorf's beneficial initiative and the governor's positive response undoubtedly saved hundreds of Jews from hunger and from further deportations. That had actually been Jagendorf's main purpose when he proposed to the Romanian governor to put his great idea into practice.[32]

When our own stock of personal belongings ran out and we had nothing more to sell, my mother, and particularly my aunts Batia and Shoshana, located acquaintances who wished to sell their possessions. My aunts took their items to the market and sold them, receiving in return a small commission from the owners. Their main clients for the purchases were the Ukrainians and the Romanian citizens who lived outside the ghetto. Aunt Batia used to take the risk of visiting Romanian homes to offer them goods. Sometimes I would accompany her on these dashes outside the ghetto, and I was astonished by the good relations that existed between my aunt and her Romanian clients. Any denouncement of us by them would have been a disaster for us. A great deal of courage was needed to secretly cross the ghetto lines, going out and in, without being noticed, to earn a small commission that turned into our main source of income.

My mother and aunt Shoshana gave a few private lessons teaching Hebrew, but this did not pay much. It happened that we received financial aid from our relatives in Czernowitz that was passed on to us by Romanian officers who often served as couriers. Much of this money 'got lost', but we did get some of it. Towards the end of our stay in the ghetto, we received additional help from the Zionist organization in Bucharest. This money, which also reached Transnistria through couriers, was distributed to Zionist activists, including my mother. Even if in financial terms this was modest assistance, it was of great psychological and moral value. The message was that we were not forgotten, and that reinforced our hope and increased our stamina in overcoming the existential problems we were facing.

I, too, with my limited strength, harnessed myself to our effort to eke out an existence. It is amazing to what an extent an 11-year-old can be considered an adult in times of distress and need. I made contact with the Jews in the ghetto who dealt in the black market, together with Romanian smugglers who frequently came to Moghilev from the other side of the Dniester. They would give packages of cigarettes, tobacco, matches, and lighters to me on credit, and I was supposed to sell them with a modest profit by strolling through the street of the ghetto and calling out the details of my wares. My hands were the 'sales counter' and my pockets shelves of stock. After I made some money this way, rather than taking items on credit, I bought them clandestinely and sold them in public openly.

Again, I was lucky I was not caught by the Romanian policemen who walked through the ghetto streets. If I had been taken, they might have tortured me to tell them the source of this merchandise, or when and how I had obtained it. In the best of cases, it would have ended up with further deportation. What could have been easier for them than to send a young Jewish boy off to hell? I remember my strong drive, really a compulsion, to take part even modestly in providing a living for my family and the dangerous initiative I took upon myself. I also well remember the sceptical looks on the faces of my mother and my aunts when they realized what kind of 'occupation' I had taken up. Their expressions reflected a lack of confidence in a boy who had suddenly become a merchant in demand, buying, and selling – and even making a profit. I kept on with my 'business' until the day of liberation, when I was 13 and a half years old.

I also did my share of the housekeeping tasks: pumping water from the well – a job solely my own – and collecting pieces of wood to be used as fuel for cooking and heating. And where did I get them from? In the vicinity of our dwelling was a large sawmill that had been in use until the German–Romanian occupation. The sawmill yard covered a large area and was guarded all day by an old watchman. When the Dniester had flooded a sizable section of Moghilev – before we were deported there – it happened that the sawmill, too, stood under water for several days. Consequently, many pieces of wood and even boards had sunk beneath the topsoil. My job and that of our neighbours was to dig in the ground and search for these buried treasures, without being caught by the watchman. This 'energy' source was inexhaustible; it supplied our needs the entire time we were in the ghetto during all seasons, especially in winter.

Beyond the modest sums of money I contributed to 'housekeeping expenses', I financed my private history lessons from Mrs Langer, a history teacher who was a deportee from Gura-Humorului, South Bucovina. History was a subject that I had liked from early boyhood. My mother taught me Hebrew literature and the Bible, and even prepared me for my Bar Mitzvah when I became 13 in December 1943. What a sad day it was for me and my family! Bar Mitzvah without my father being there and in the shadow of destruction? I went to the makeshift synagogue on a weekday in the company of a family friend, Advocate Simcha Sobe.[33] He taught me how to put on *tefillin* for the first time on the morning of my Bar Mitzvah day during the morning prayers. The worshipers looked at me in surprise. Why does a young Jewish boy facing the threat of death every minute need to learn to put on *tefillin*? Or, for that matter, to learn history or Bible, to sing 'Hatikva' and 'Techezakna'?[34] To solve arithmetic exercises with his aunt Shoshana? Is there any greater absurdity?

Years later, when looking for an answer to these questions, I thought in terms of today: Perhaps this was an expression of spiritual resistance by the Jews in the ghettos? Or a means to survive? Or an attempt to escape from the tragic reality of daily life in which we were steeped? Perhaps the power of intellectual curiosity? Or could it be faith in tomorrow and the instinctive need to be prepared for it?

The communal organization of the Moghilev ghetto was amazing, considering the circumstances. It had begun as early as the first stages, with the arrival of the Bucovina deportee convoys in Moghilev, and continued more energetically after the establishment of the ghetto in town. Demanded was a supreme effort, a lot of wisdom, and, above all, the talent of local leadership to exploit the potential existing with all the physicians, nurses, engineers, and teachers available towards the creation of a basis for social, educational, and cultural life and welfare-support services under the sub-human conditions prevailing in the ghetto. This became particularly pressing after the raging typhus epidemic that killed thousands. It was also necessary to obtain the assistance of the remaining Jews in Romania – with Antonescu's approval – to receive medicines as well as financial aid for the upkeep of the hospital, three orphanages, a school, and a soup kitchen for those totally destitute. Although the aid from the 'Rescue Committee' and from the 'Jews Centre' in Bucharest[35] did not arrive immediately, and even though it was never enough to cover vital needs, and despite the imperfections of the welfare institutions owing to the lack of sufficient financial resources, these institutions forged a most important existential infrastructure in the ghetto. Another aspect of activity by the leaders of the 'Jewish Committee' in the ghetto was their conducting fateful negotiations with the Romanian administration on the abolition of the harsh deportation decrees, or at least to limit their scope considerably. Did they succeed?

Rumours circulated claiming that, from time to time, the Jewish leadership of the ghetto would bribe the Romanian governor and his assistants with a great deal of money to obtain residence permits for the deportees in Moghilev and to reduce the scope of deportations from there eastwards. At the same time, the Jewish leadership strived hard to convince the governor of the vital value of ghetto Jews for carrying out urgent tasks and performing skilled craftsmanship needed by the occupying authorities. Moreover, the mere fact that the 'Jewish Committee' leaders consented to deportations eastwards from Moghilev – even if they were negotiating to limit them – laid the basis for cooperation between them and the authorities for all aspects of deportations. From this point of view, one may assume there was no great difference between the Jewish leadership of Moghilev and that of the Judenrat in Nazi-occupied Europe (about whom we learned after the war). If we judge, however, by our feelings in those days, the Moghilev ghetto Jewish leadership seems to have played a most important role through their negotiations with the occupying authorities, whether by bribing them, or by obtaining aid – with their approval or, at times, through their offices – from the Jews Centre in Bucharest. Therein lies the difference between the Jewish Committee and the Judenrat.

The 'Jewish Committee' of the Moghilev ghetto – considered, as we learned after the war, the largest ghetto in Transnistria, with its survivors numbering about ten thousnad – was undoubtedly aware of the tremendous responsibility it had taken upon itself. The authorities repeatedly demanded supplying them with a certain quota of people destined for deportation, and the committee was ultimately forced, during each *aktzia* that took place in the ghetto, to give its consent to the deportations, without its being directly involved in selecting deportees. To fill the quotas the Romanian Gendarmerie would kidnap deportees who did not have permits to stay in Moghilev from the street or their dwellings. Whoever managed to hide in time was saved. The Jewish policemen who acted on behalf of the Jewish Committee assisted the Gendarmerie more passively than actively. Still the Jewish Committee leaders understood the scope of the *aktzias.* They bargained with the authorities on the magnitude of the deportation quota. In most instances they did succeed in reducing it, but they were finally forced to give in. There may have been some kind of tacit agreement that allowed residence permit holders to remain in town. Who knows?

Of course the Jewish Committee could not prevent the deportation from the Moghilev ghetto to the concentration camps Scazinetz, Lutchinetz, Shargorod, Kopayegrod, and worst of all, Peciora – considered a death camp. But at the same time the committee was probably well aware that any number – small or large – of deportees saved from further deportation was an important achievement. Dozens of families deported from Moghilev managed to run away and return to the ghetto in town, amongst them people from our town, Edinitz: Liza and Matityahu Koifman, who fled Scazinetz, and the Fragis family, deported across the Bug river, who had been assisted by a local Ukrainian family that had also hidden their small son when there had been a *kinder aktzia* – a round-up of children to be sent off to their deaths at the hands of the Germans. Among those who returned to Moghilev were members of the Kunis family who had sheltered us when we slipped away from the deportees' convoy the morning after our arrival in Moghilev. We heard of no case of the Jewish Committee leaders turning in any returnee to the ghetto who did not have a local residence permit. Had that happened, I think we would have known. At any rate, the interaction of the Jewish Committee with the occupying authorities aimed not only at minimizing deportation quotas, but also at increasing the number of Moghilev residence permits by proving to them that the deportees were indispensable. And in that, they were quite successful.

Two other achievements of the Jewish Committee stand out in my memory: the establishment of an orphanage in the ghetto (April 1942; eventually two more were set up) and the organization of a school that went through fourth grade and functioned separately from schooling at the orphanages. The thousands of deportees who perished along the *via dolorosa* to Transnistria as well as in Moghilev itself from hunger and typhus left behind thousands of homeless orphans with no means of subsistence. They aimlessly walked the ghetto streets, barefoot, ragged, utterly silent, self-absorbed, covered with running sores. Their deep eyes looked out from sad, wrinkled faces; they were hungry for a piece of bread and a drop of human warmth. They were terrifying to look at, walking skeletons. When any of them stopped near our house, where many families lived, we would give them some bread from the little we had without saying a word. Gathering hundreds of orphans into a shelter was considered a great deed, even if at first they were only served a poor meal once a day, one that could not quiet their hunger. They continued to roam the streets of the ghetto, but at least now they were under the supervision of physicians, nurses, and teachers. Rumours circulated that their death rate had declined but not to the minimum. When aid from the Rescue Committee and the Jews Centre began to reach the ghetto regularly, both money and medicine, the orphans' situation improved considerably.

Their redemption from Hell began when the Jews Centre in Bucharest and Dr W. Filderman, former chairman of the Federation of Jewish Communities in Romania, succeeded in obtaining from the Romanian authorities – after investing great effort and lobbying for over a year – permission to transfer orphans from Transnistria to the care of Jewish communities in the Moldova region in Romania. This was shortly before the liberation of Transnistria by the Red Army.

Dr Filderman himself had been deported in summer 1943

from Bucharest to the Moghilev Ghetto for several months at Antonescu's order because of his refusal to pay a large amount of money as a contribution to the Romanian authorities on behalf of the Jewish communities of Romania. During the course of his deportation in Moghilev, he could see for himself the frightfully desperate situation of the deportees in general, and of the orphans in particular. I remember that he settled with his wife into a large building opposite the Turnatoria, with people lining up near his residence from early morning to late evening to meet him and tell him about their pressing problems. For Filderman this was an excellent opportunity to become familiar with the intolerable living conditions of the deportees. From this point of view, more than the punishment Antonescu had intended for him, this step inadvertently provided Filderman with an unexpected chance to see the actual situation. In my eyes, and those of many other deportees, he was seen as king of the Jews and as a source of salvation who contributed greatly to alleviating our suffering. We were saddened to hear that he was about to return to Bucharest; he had been an inspiration for confidence in the future. We consoled ourselves by thinking that from Bucharest he might be able to do more to save us than from the Moghilev ghetto. We had great faith in him and hoped he would not disappoint us. And he did not.

We heard about his initiatives and indefatigable effort to prevent the deportation of Jews from other parts of Romanian territory in general and, in particular, to return surviving deportees from Transnistria to their homes in Bessarabia, Bucovina, and the Dorohoi district, while constantly acting to improve their economic situation while they were still in Transnistria. During our deportation and well afterwards I considered him one of the most able and bravest Jewish leaders who had a striking effect during the Holocaust. His unique personality and outstanding courage found particular expression in his desperate negotiations with Antonescu and his cabinet ministers, with his high moral stance and national pride frequently endangering his own life.[36]

The educational system in the orphanages played an important role in reinforcing a mind-set for survival. I became acquainted only with the first orphanage, the oldest and the largest among the three. I did not get to know it well, since I was never a pupil at the lessons given there. It was mainly when the orphanage students performed on the occasion of our Jewish holidays that I, along with other young people my age and adults, visited there. The repertoire was taken mainly from life in the ghetto. The sketches had some humour to them, and whoever saw them left uplifted, full of admiration for these young actors' talents. In addition to the short plays, the presentations included songs and recitations, in Yiddish and Hebrew, expressing sadness and desperation but also the hope to reach Eretz Israel some day.

Another school, an independent one, also only for the first four grades, was founded with the help of Turnatoria. The pupils were mainly the sons and daughters of the foundry workers. Some of my friends joined them, even though they were not in that category. Since I had already finished fourth grade and was busy selling my 'merchandise' in the ghetto streets many hours a day, I had no interest in studying with them. I knew the school only from hearsay. The pedagogical approach of the teachers perhaps leaned towards working with a more organized set of studies than the one followed in the orphanages where the attitude towards pupils was more liberal and family-like. In both cases, however, the teachers used no textbook or any other teaching aids, since there were none. Consequently the teachers had to invest great effort in teaching arithmetic, literature, history, and Hebrew language, everything based on their own knowledge. In both types of schools, but particularly in the orphanages, a national-Zionist spirit prevailed, characterized by the desire to emigrate one day to Eretz Israel.[37]

We played very little. We were much too serious for that, but here and there we invented games. One of them consisted of a list of capital cities all over the world where we would like to live in the future – as if we were not living with a noose resting lightly around our neck, not knowing what our fate would be the next hour. In the next column were squares standing beside the city names. Each city was given a number, and each player counted the number of squares he had been assigned. The last capital to be matched to its number was the one we would live in, 'when we will be grown ups'. Most of the time in the game 'Jerusalem' turned up for me. Apparently this was the city where I always wanted to live. Amazingly, this became reality. This game was a combination of geographical knowledge and a great deal of optimism and imagination.

We loved to talk about the few books we happened to come across and which we read avidly. We tried to imagine for ourselves how we would have acted in place of the main figure of the story. Sometimes we would conduct a mock trial of the books heroes – who was guilty, who was innocent. On such work that stirred lively debate among us was *The Defense Speaks Out*; I don't remember who wrote it. But I do recall that the story takes place in a whorehouse. The author's purpose was to put society on trial as forcing women into this ancient profession. No other book we had at that time had such a great influence over us, personifying as it were the confrontation and interdependency between the individual and society.

Among my friends in the ghetto was a young girl my age who lived in our neighbourhood. We saw each other almost every day, whether in the houses we were living in – where many people were crowded together – or at gatherings of our friends. Both of us were on the threshold of adolescence. She was attractive, and gradually won my heart. I went through sleepless nights over her, but I was shy and very careful not to display any of my feelings for her. She never even knew about them. Or, if she had guessed or sensed what was going on, she never showed she was aware of them. After the liberation, our paths separated. Although many years have passed, the remembrance of my first love, in the shadow of destruction, remains engraved in my memory.

Social life for my mother and her two sisters was limited to the circle of our neighbours and a few close friends who lived nearby. Whenever I happened to sit in on their conversations the predominant topics were always the days gone by – naturally accompanied by a great deal of nostalgia – and, of course, the news of the day. Sometimes they would sing songs from the 'old days', but also sad songs portraying life in the ghetto and the longing for a normal life once again. A song I particularly remember, one I really liked to hear and even to sing by myself, in Yiddish, is called 'Maybe'. Here is a free translation of its words:

> Maybe I built my fortresses in the air,
> Maybe my God does not exist,
> In my dream, I feel better, in my dream, it is nicer,
> In my dream the sky is bluer than blue.
>
> Maybe I will never reach my goal,
> Maybe my ship will never reach its shore,
> I do not mind if I do not manage to reach it,
> All I want is to move towards it along a sunny way.

(At that time I did not know who wrote the poem or composed the song, but not long ago my friend Tova Ben-Zvi told me that it was I. Papernikov who did so shortly before the First World War broke out. He emigrated to Israel and she knew him well. Tova, who researched and collected songs sung in the ghettos and concentration camps – many of which are in her repertoire as a singer – told me that 'Maybe' was sung in other ghettos, too.)

Included in our circle of friends in Moghilev was Dr Alma Tennenbaum – called Buschka by her friends – a deportee (like ourselves) from Czernowitz. She was an exceptional personality on the human scene of the ghetto. Day and night she devoted herself to curing the ill, in the ghetto and in the surrounding Ukrainian villages (we never knew how she got there). She used to visit us frequently, always bringing some fresh eggs – which she received in return for giving medical treatment – and they were earmarked for me, she said, since I was on the threshold of adulthood and needed good food to insure my growth. Indeed, those eggs, along with some other food items Buschka brought us, helped me overcome the chronic shortage of food and lack of vitamins so necessary for my existence. She also obtained – God knows how – injections of the medicine that cured me of the pus-oozing sores that covered my neck. She possessed a great deal of idealism and good faith in our being liberated shortly by the Red Army and in the collapse of Nazism in Europe. I had a suspicion – which in time turned out to be true – that she had contacts with the partisan underground through the connections she had made in the Ukrainian villages in Moghilev's surrounding area. She never spoke of this. Had she been caught by the Romanian Gendarmerie she would probably have been executed. Shortly after liberation she arranged for us to cross the Dniester westwards through Ataki by means of the good offices of a Soviet army officer. From there we continued on our own, hitchhiking to Edinitz. Dr Tennenbaum's noble personality and the wonderful acts she performed for us in those distressing times in the Moghilev ghetto are deeply etched in my memory.

Many years later I met her in Vienna when I was serving as Israel's ambassador to Austria. Her charm and sense of humour had weathered well, even though she was then over 90. She told me on that occasion, among other things, that shortly after the liberation she had voluntarily joined the Red Army, serving as a physician. She had advanced with the army westwards, reaching Vienna, and there she had stayed permanently. I also found out that she was a member of the Communist Party, while at the same time avidly following Jewish affairs, even visiting Israel several times. She passed away in 1997 (a year after I completed my diplomatic mission in Austria), but not before she had made a significant contribution to the building of a central hall at the Ghetto Fighters Museum in the Yad Layeled (Memorial for the Child) pavilion, named after Janos Korczak.

In the evenings my mother and my two aunts used to read the Romanian newspapers that we managed to get from Romanian civilians who were working in Moghilev, either with the Romanian governor or at the railway station administered by Romanian officers and technicians. In the absence of electricity or a kerosene lamp, we used to scoop out a potato and fill the shell with a little bit of oil, put a thread in as a wick, and light it. This was all the light we had for night-time reading of newspapers or of books that sometimes passed from hand to hand.

From the newspapers that reached the deportees we found out about the harsh battles at Stalingrad and of the gradual advancement westwards of the Red Army. Full pages of the Romanian papers were devoted to photos of fallen Romanian soldiers and descriptions of their brave acts. At that time, I naively thought to myself who knows how many of them had taken part in the mass killings of Jews in Bessarabia and North Bucovina, in the acts of violence, the raping of young girls, and the looting on their way to the front. The truth is that I was not sorry they had fallen.

We and our neighbours would reconstruct each battle, thirsting to know how it would end. We got our answer at a later stage, whenever 'fresh' Romanian newspapers happened to come our way. Lacking any other means of communication, the news would circulate from mouth to ear. As the front moved closer to Moghilev, our hopes for rescue grew stronger. Further reinforcement came for the repeated rumours that the Romanian authorities were going to allow surviving deportees to return to their homes. At first the idea was received hesitantly, but when such permission was actually given to a number of families deported from Dorohoi, the rumours took on substantial meaning. For us, however, this was not to be. Only after the Red Army liberated us did our return become possible.

Years after the war we learned about the exhausting negotiations that Dr Filderman and other delegates of the Jewish community of Bucharest had carried out with the representatives of the Antonescu administration about the return from Transnistria of 70,000 deportees. Jewish Agency representatives in Istanbul were also involved in these dialogues. According to rumours rife in Moghilev, the idea was to allow the refugees to sail to Eretz Israel on boats hired by the Jewish Agency, rather than to have them return to their homes. The fact that the Yishuv (the Jewish population in pre-state Israel) was involved in the fate of the Transnistria deportees and the need to rescue them and bring them safely to the shores of Eretz Israel was for us – and I presume for all Transnistria survivors – a belated consolation, even if it never came to pass. I am still puzzled today as to why Antonescu instructed his assistants to conduct such negotiations. Was he seriously thinking about such a move? Was it the money promised to him, if this project were put into motion? Or was it that he sensed the approaching, crashing defeat of Hitler's and Romania's troops in the battles against the Soviet Union and thought a gesture of good will towards the Jews would stand to his credit when judgement day arrived?

Israeli historians have grappled with this issue, but I feel they have reached no definite conclusion.[38] Even if the project for returning the deportees to Romania never came into being, another one did: the return of the orphans from Transnistria to Romania in what seemed a heaven-sent miracle. As mentioned earlier, several months before the liberation the Romanian authorities enabled the evacuation of the orphaned children from the ghettos of Transnistria, including the Moghilev ghetto, to the remaining Jewish communities in Romania. At the time, this seemed like a dream that would be difficult to make come true. When the clearing out of the Moghilev orphanages began, it was suggested that I join them, even though my status as an orphan was unclear since we did not know my father's fate. Moreover, the Romanian authorities insisted in not including in the evacuation children who still had one living parent. Yet there were some exceptions. My mother did her best to persuade me to go along with them. People thought that this was a sure way of being saved. I simply refused. I argued that whatever was going to happen to my mother and my aunts would apply to me, too. I was part and parcel of them and vice versa. I did not think it was right to separate myself from them after all we had been through together. Maybe my digging in my heels was illogical, since the prevailing notion was 'Whoever can save himself from this hell should do so!' But, still, I felt that in rescuing myself I would be abandoning them, and in the battle between logic and emotion, emotion won.

Years later I asked myself from where did I draw the strength and stamina to so determinedly insist on not being evacuated from the hell of Transnistria? I found the answer in the mutual devotion and sacrifice that had characterized so much of our common lives under the shadow of destruction. Leaving my family for my own benefit seemed to me an act of treason. Had I faced a similar dilemma as an adult – rather than as a youngster – I would have behaved exactly the same.

Nearly 2,000 orphans were evacuated from Transnistria.[39] About five months after their dispersal among the Jewish communities in the Moldova area, 60 of them – together with 300 Jewish refugees from Romania – set out on the immigrant ship *Mefkure*, which was torpedoed and sunk by the Germans on 4 August 1944 in the Black Sea, two days after it had sailed from the Romanian port Constanta in the direction of Haifa – illegally. Only five refugees were miraculously rescued. All the rest, including the orphans, drowned at sea. What a terrible tragedy: to be saved from the hands of the Nazis and from the threat of hunger and illness and to begin the rehabilitation process among the Jewish communities who cared so devotedly for the needs of those 60 orphans, and to be privileged to be included among those departing for the 'safe' shores of Eretz Israel, and then, when just on the threshold of realizing great hopes and expectations for their young lives, to be drowned in the Black Sea, again by the long arm of Nazi Germany. Was their fate determined in Heaven? God knows!

Today, when I think of the story of the Jewish orphans saved in the Moghilev ghetto as well as in other Transnistria ghettos (the total number of orphans in all of Transnistria before the liberation is estimated at some 8,000, among them 1,600 from Moghilev) in which orphanages were founded at the initiative of the deportees' Jewish Committees and with the help of Jewish institutions in Bucharest, I can identify characteristics that are, perhaps, unique in the history of the Holocaust in those years.

1. The wisdom and resourcefulness of the committee leaders to begin the campaign to rescue the orphans from hunger, exhaustion, and illness – at first with local help and afterwards with outside assistance – by constantly pressuring the Rescue Committee and the Bucharest Jews Centre to move swiftly to save them.
2. The endless devotion of physicians, nurses, and educators in granting the orphans shelter, curing them from illness to the extent possible in the absence of hygienic conditions and medicines, and feeding them, even if only in small quantities, reduced the death rate appreciably and provided them an intimate family atmosphere in the orphanages and a learning atmosphere imbued with national spirit, all of which kept up their morale and gave them hope for redemption from the Transnistrian hell on their way to Eretz Israel.
3. The great miracle that half of Romania's Jews were not deported and were thus saved from the Holocaust. And the extension of that miracle: that those who remained in their homes could provide large amounts of material and financial aid to the Transnistria deportees as well as conduct negotiations with the authorities in a manner unmatched anywhere else in Europe under the Nazi regime.
4. The resourcefulness of the Jewish leaders in Bucharest in putting pressure on the Romanian authorities, either directly or through the International Red Cross, the Vatican, and the foreign ambassadors serving in Bucharest, to ease the sufferings of the deportees and thwart German

pressure on Antonescu to deport the remainder, the second half, of Romania's Jews to the concentration and death camps of Poland. This kind of activity developed in the course of Antonescu's disappointments from the results of the war against the Soviet Union, and his fear that one day he would be tried for his war crimes. Undoubtedly, it had a positive influence on his political considerations concerning the fate of Romania's Jews in general and that of the deportees in Transnistria in particular. This also sheds light on his agreeing to transfer the orphans from Transnistria to the Moldova area of Romania and decreeing that deportees could return to their homes. He announced his permission a few days before the Soviet–German front neared the borders of Romania, but nothing came of it since time ran out for him. In practical terms this permission was irrelevant, but in principle it was uniquely important.

5. The behaviour of the Jewish leadership in the ghettos of Transnistria and in Bucharest could serve as an example of leadership in any acute crisis.

The combination of all these factors lent a unique character to the Transnistria deportees in general and to the orphans there, in particular.

It is to be hoped that history will not let the Romanian people forget that during the fascist period in their country, its sons, soldiers, and commanders murdered and executed, starved, humiliated, and tortured tens of thousands of Jews in Bessarabia, Bucovina, and the Dorohoi district *before deporting them* to Transnistria, during the deportation, and even well afterwards on the explicit order of the tyrant Antonescu. In addition, they perpetrated mass murders of Jews in occupied Ukraine and the pogroms of Bucharest (1941) and Iasi (1941). One must keep in mind, however, that half of Romania's Jews were saved from deportation under that same fascist regime that then prevailed in Romania.

5 Liberation, Homecoming, and Victory Day

The liberation arrived dramatically. Red Army soldiers reached the outskirts of Moghilev on 23 March 1944.

Several days earlier low-flying German military aircraft had frequently circled around Moghilev. They did not bomb the town. Perhaps they were looking for partisans, the advance guard of the Red Army, or for Soviet military concentrations.

Also during that period German soldiers – based that month in Moghilev – paid surprise visits to the ghetto. It happened to us, too. German soldiers ordered all the inhabitants of our apartment house to leave their rooms and form a circle outside the building. We thought that our lives had come to an end. Fear was rife in the ghetto that the Germans would annihilate the surviving Jews of the ghetto before their retreat from the town. Every time the German soldiers took us outside, we bid each other goodbye with a swift look. To our good fortune, the nightmare finally ended with a spine-chilling identification inspection. Were they searching for partisans? Had they given up the idea of murdering the Jews?

At night the bridges over the Dniester were exploded. The next morning the German military vehicles suspended on the remnants of the bridges could be clearly seen. The bombings were probably a partisan campaign to prevent German retreat westward and to take the Germans prisoner along with their military equipment. The opposite view held that the Germans were the perpetrators in an attempt to delay the Red Army's advancement westward. But across the Dniester, on its western side, German snipers took shelter and shot towards Moghilev, particularly aiming at the ghetto.

In the days between the German retreat (the Romanian soldiers were long gone) and the Red Army's entry into Moghilev, many people in the ghetto shut themselves up in their houses. Bullets from across the river whistled past on every side, and stepping out was a dangerous act. I took the risk of leaving our building believing that nothing would happen to me. Fortunately the whizzing bullets did not hit me. Much to our sorrow, however, they did strike some of our neighbours who had ventured out, as I had, into the ghetto streets. What a cruel fate, to make it through to liberation day only to be killed by a German sniper across the river!

My going out into the streets had not been vital and, considering the circumstances, rather foolish. But I just had to see the soldiers of the Red Army entering the ghetto and greet them with cheers as our saviours and redeemers. Wasn't this the day we had been waiting for after nearly three years of Nazi occupation, from the conquest by the German and Romanian armies in July 1941 up to the fear-ridden, anguish-laden past few hours? Many of us were looking forward to this day, and so many others had been less fortunate. How could I stay shut up in our small room on such a day and not stretch out a warm and friendly hand to our liberators, whom we saw as the greatest strike force in the war to dismantle the Nazi regime? (Being cut off from sources of information we were unaware of the British and American participation in the fight against Nazi Germany. We only learned of this after liberation, and it took another year until we learned of the existence of the Jewish Brigade.)

The main street of the ghetto, Ulitsa Poltavskaya, to which the German bullets had not penetrated, usually reverberated with the noise of people on the move. Now it was totally still. Here and there I saw Soviet soldiers, running with guns in hand in search of shelter. They did not have a moment for celebrations of welcome or for greetings and salutations.

Seated in the middle of the street, leaning on a fence, was a group of unarmed German soldiers, dressed in ragged uniforms and looking humiliated, actually waiting to be taken prisoner. This scene was beyond imagination: German soldiers, yesterday's conquerors, now waiting helplessly, poor and miserable. I felt such pity for them that I was almost moved to put my hand in my pocket to take out a coin and give it to them to help them survive. As far as I remember I had no feelings of revenge, nor did the other Jews with me at this tableau. No one made a move to kill them. It was as if all the hatred we felt for the Germans had melted away. Maybe just seeing them so pitiful was our sweet revenge. Perhaps – and this I think is the main point – we had no inkling then of the extent of the extermination of Jews by the Germans in Poland, Germany, Austria, Ukraine, Belorussia, the Baltic states, and so many other places.

The Red Army entry was purposeful, straight to the point, without ceremonies or festivities. A lot of work had to be done. First was the need to put up a bridge over the Dniester in the shortest possible time. Without the bridge there would be no way to move military equipment towards the front, even if the infantry could cross the river in boats. Soviet soldiers worked day and night on rebuilding the bridge with the help of volunteers taken from their homes by the soldiers. Second came the immediate registration of the men for purposes of mobilization, including the exhausted Jews just liberated from occupation.

The Soviet corps of engineers had the other bridges back in use in a very short time. In less than two weeks heavy military vehicles and equipment were rolling across the bridges towards the front that had moved further and further westwards from us – with no German interference from the air.

The rate of the mobilization campaign increased. Some of our acquaintances among the recruited were sent towards the front on a train that was bombed by the German air force. They never returned to their families. Again, the tragic fate of the Jews: to have been saved from the Holocaust only to be killed by German bombardment just a few weeks after liberation by the Red Army.

Although a free way of life returned to Moghilev, the town went through radical changes during the first three months of the Soviet regime settling in there in all domains. A new administration was set up that was adapted to muster all resources for the war; the first move it made carrying out arrests among the Ukrainian population of individuals who had cooperated with the German and Romanian occupation authorities. Much to our regret and disappointment, the Soviets also arrested several leaders of the Jewish community (formerly, the ghetto) on the basis of the same suspicion. Yet the only 'crime' of the Jewish leaders was that they had negotiated with the Romanian administration for the abolishment of decrees calling for further deportations and for the guarantee of normal functioning of the ghetto welfare institutions.

'GOING HOME'

About two months after liberation we decided to set out for home. The war was still being fiercely waged along the Prut River (that separates Bessarabia and North Bucovina from Romania), when survivors – including us – from all over Transnistria began to 'return home', to start a new life, whether it be in their previous place of residence or elsewhere.

My mother and I went to Edinitz. We were greatly concerned about my father's fate, and we expected him to come back to Edinitz after three years of separation. We knew nothing about him except for the crumbs of information we had collected upon our arrival in Moghilev from people who had escaped the deportee convoy while marching through the Moghilev streets. Our hope was that he, too, had managed to survive the hell to which we had been deported separately.

My aunts Batia and Shoshana, with whom we had survived three years of deportation in the Moghilev ghetto, left for Czernowitz. (Waiting for them there were my uncle, who had been safely released from his forced labour camp, and other family members who had successfully remained in Czernowitz during the German–Romanian occupation.)

The return to Edinitz after all that had happened was extremely traumatic. The remnants of Edinitz families who had begun to return 'home' from all liberated parts of Transnistria needed supreme effort, physical and spiritual, to overcome all the difficulties involved. Only 200–300 Jews out of 6,000 Jewish inhabitants survived the Holocaust. It seems to me that only the encouraging news reaching us from the front lines about the retreating German army gave us the courage and the will to reintegrate into daily life.

The survivors who slowly made it back to Edinitz renewed the Jewish settlement in the town. They carried in their hearts all the horrifying memories of what they had seen from the moment of occupation to the moment of liberation; they remained witnesses to annihilation. During the ten months of our stay in Edinitz, and I assume for a long time afterwards, they would talk of what had happened to this one or that, and the answers given were 'died', 'burned', 'murdered', 'buried (alive)', 'perished', or had 'disappeared'. My father was among the 'disappeared'. As I have mentioned before, he was taken one morning by Romanian soldiers to work together with another group of men at the Vertujeni camp. None of them came back, none of them was ever seen after that morning. Now and then a spot of light would glimmer when we found out that a relative, friend, acquaintance, or neighbour had survived the Holocaust. The tragedy of annihilation that had affected every survivor was almost more than each could bear. Only the impetus for life gave some relief to their searing pain.

The war went on for another year after the return of the survivors to Edinitz.[40] Their economic and spiritual rehabilitation proceeded slowly. Only a small part of their homes had been destroyed. The majority of Jewish homes had been occupied by the local, Christian population shortly after the owner's deportation. Great were the sorrow and pain when passing a house of a relative, friend, or acquaintance who had perished in the Holocaust and seeing that it had been inherited by others, probably with all of its contents. The local population was ordered to evacuate the homes of the returning survivors. Part of them did vacate the occupied Jewish houses even before the survivors' return – as was the case with our house – for fear, probably, that they would be punished by the Soviet authorities if they did not do so. For quite some time the returning survivors were involved with redeeming their homes and other property from the local Christian population, whether it be from those who occupied their houses, or from passers-by who were wearing clothes they recognized as their own, or whether in conducting their own investigation. The Soviet authorities usually helped the Jews reclaim their property.

Another type of cooperation between the survivors and the local authorities was in the bringing to justice of collaborators with the German and Romanian occupying forces. They were the individuals who had participated in the mass murders of Jews immediately upon the entry into Edinitz of the invading forces. Those caught who were tried and convicted were sentenced to 20–30 years of hard labour.

Since the local and district authorities considered the survivors reliable and intelligent, they gave them responsible jobs and functions in the local administration – a fact that contributed to the process of their reintegration into daily life.

It was only natural that the survivors would prefer to live near one another. In some cases people whose homes had been destroyed during their period of deportation moved into houses owned by Jews known to have perished in the Holocaust. Thus, in the early period, returning survivors lived once again in a concentrated section that had been known before the war as a Jewish area. The close proximity of Jewish dwellings strengthened the sense of security, more than before. At first small-scale trade flourished, led by a considerable percentage of the survivors. This soon came to an end.

No effort was made to set up a Jewish community. Such an institution was not founded even later, when the number of Jews increased slightly.

As early as the beginning of the school year in September 1944 two main schools were established in Edinitz. In the first school all subjects in the curriculum were taught in Russian, in the other school, in Moldavian. The Jewish pupils preferred the Russian school, where they were a prominent minority. No attempt was made to set up a Yiddish school, as had been done during the Soviet rule in 1940–41. First of all, in contrast to the past, the number of Jewish pupils amongst the survivors was very low. Second, the means for such a school were lacking: the small number of Jewish teachers among the survivors was insufficient for carrying out such a mission; teachers who could teach in Yiddish were not brought from the Soviet Union; and Yiddish textbooks were not available. Under those circumstances the authorities did not show any interest in creating a Yiddish school or even in assisting putting such a project into motion.

The educational level of the Jewish pupils was, understandably, relatively quite low. Three years of wandering and deportation had deprived them of the opportunity for studying a conventional, normal curriculum. The Jewish pupils were accepted into classes at the school on the basis of their level of limited knowledge, although the authorities did take their age into consideration, too. That meant – as in my case – there was difference of two or three years between the Jewish and non-Jewish pupils. The Jewish pupils worked hard to close the gap in their knowledge, including the study of Russian. Within a fairly short period, they distinguished themselves at school.

Little by little films trickled into the town – the majority with war themes – and books, mainly Russian literature, both classical and contemporary (generally describing events involving the horrors of war and or acts of bravery by individuals, at the front or in the rear). Theatrical performances and song concerts were held from time to time, as well. All these helped survivors re-enter local life.

There was a lack of intellectual manpower. To make up for this, in many cases people were trained in short courses. Moreover, the Soviet teachers who came to Edinitz from the territories of the Soviet Union on a pedagogical mission made a considerable contribution to local cultural life, and the school soon became an important centre of cultural revival.

Jews felt deep appreciation and gratitude towards the liberating Red Army. The front moved further and further away, and it seems that for us, with all our grief and sorrow, there was no greater joy than hearing news of the German defeat in battles. Reports also spread among the Jews of Edinitz about the brave acts of local Jewish soldiers who had joined the Red Army in the fight against the Nazis. Towards the end of August 1944 we heard about the Romanian army – until then fighting together with the Germans against the Soviet Union – now joining the Allied Forces in their fight against Germany. Initially received as somewhat suspicious, it ultimately proved true. For the local hostile Moldavian population, this was a huge blow, but for the Jews it was a source of joy.

Several weeks after our return to Edinitz we moved into our house. The Christians who had been living there during the occupation had left it shortly before we returned. The house was in good order, and we even found some of our furniture – they probably hadn't had time to take it with them. The feeling of entering the almost empty house, without my father, was terrible. I saw him everywhere. Even if the chances of seeing him return alive were almost nil, we did not stop hoping that 'here he comes'. Even though we tried to find out more about him from eyewitnesses, we did not gain any information beyond what we already had.

In the summertime I used to buy fruit at wholesale prices and sell it in the market at retail. This was a good source of income. I was already 13-and-a-half years old, and had developed a good sense of trade.

With the beginning of the school year I was accepted into sixth grade. Although going to school had never been the joy of my life, I must admit that I liked it very much, especially the teachers who came from the Soviet Union to teach us. They devoted themselves wholeheartedly to each individual pupil, particularly the Jewish ones.

My mother gave private lessons teaching Russian, even though she was not an expert in this language. She was sufficiently proficient, however, to teach it, and with her pedagogical approach she did it very well and was much appreciated. She did not want to accept a teaching position in the school for fear that she would not be released from a job as a teacher – as was the custom in the Soviet Union – in case we decided to leave Edinitz.

In the absence of any news about my father, our suspicion that we would not be seeing him again turned into more and more of a certainty. However, we suppressed this notion in our minds and never did stop hoping that one bright day he would return to us. And so, two months before the end of the war, March 1945, we left Edinitz to join our family in Czernowitz. We lived for about a year in their apartment until we, all of us, could continue on our way to Eretz Israel. We let our house in Edinitz to a Jewish teacher, a Holocaust survivor, and at a later stage we sold it.

When I said goodbye to Edinitz it was as if I was released from a heavy burden. Every time I met a local resident while walking in the street or anywhere else, I could not help thinking that perhaps this was someone who had assisted the Romanian soldiers in killing the local Jews when the German and Romanian soldiers captured Edinitz in early July 1941. Whenever I passed a house that had belonged to any of our relatives, friends, or acquaintances who were no more, I saw them standing before me as if they were alive. The same was true for the teachers of my destroyed school and for dozens of my schoolmates who had left this world in torment and pain – here they were, gazing at me from every corner, every side, deploring pleading with me to never forget them.

VICTORY DAY

Victory Day over Nazi Germany, 9 May 1945, found us in Czernowitz. Several weeks earlier I had fallen ill and become bedridden. A physician – a friend of ours – diagnozed this as serious malnutrition (as a result of the Holocaust years). He tried to make up for my shortage of calcium and vitamins by injecting them in large doses. I was extremely weak and could hardly walk. Nevertheless, on 10 May, when Red Army soldiers were parading in the city's main street, on which we lived, I summoned enough strength to go out to watch the parade and listen to the soldier's beloved patriotic victory songs. Their singing was quite faint. I followed after them with great difficulty. It looked to me as though they could hardly pick up their feet to march, just as I could hardly lift mine. God knows how many places they had marched through in their short lives during the war years until the arrival of this historic day that we had all been waiting for so long. Yet, instead of feelings of joy and happiness stirring in my heart – as expected on such a day – I suddenly grasped, as a boy turned adolescent, the enormity of the destruction, the orphanhood, the bereavement, the magnitude of the devastation we had experienced all those years from the day we were expelled to the ghetto from the same street on which I was now following the marching Red Army soldiers, as tired and exhausted as I was. It was only on this day that I realized the immense destruction wrought by the war and the Holocaust years. It was a very personal experience. Only then did I understand my orphanhood. Perhaps, because I had not seen with my own eyes the bitter end of my father's life, hope always remained in my heart that we would meet again. And now, here was Victory Day, my father was no more, and who knew how many more had perished. I saw the ruins of war much more realistically than I had seen them before. The destruction and devastation had been around me day and night, but only on Victory Day did I fully grasp the significance, a day that remains engraved in my memory but not exactly as a day of celebration.

During the victory year 1945–46, I went through a process of readjustment to the norms of life in the post-war period and of physical rehabilitation to bring my poor health back to normal. We were assisted by my uncle and aunt, in whose apartment we were living and who fortunately had not been deported to Transnistria and had not gone through the hell we had experienced. Actually this was a return to the apartment from which we had been expelled to the ghetto, and which I had always considered to be my second home, the first being in Edinitz.

Yet, unlike our return to Edinitz shortly after the liberation, in Czernowitz we found a Jewish community following its normal way of life, despite the many restrictions imposed on it by the Romanian fascist regime. Although this situation made it easier for me to enter the readjustment process to the norms of my new life, I found myself in psychological confrontation with Jewish boys my age, who had spent the war years in Czernowitz and who had no clue to what we had gone through in Transnistria. Even when I tried to become part of their society, I felt that we were strangers to each other. Their interests differed from mine, and their outlook on life took another slant. Theirs was normal, mine very much influenced by life in the shadow of destruction. Beyond that, the gap between their knowledge and mine set me back at least two years in comparison to them. Since my schooling in Edinitz had been interrupted in sixth grade with our move to Czernowitz, I now began to work by myself to make up all the material needed for me to be accepted into seventh grade in the Yiddish state school in Czernowitz, at the beginning of the 1945/46 school year.

I became an avid reader, devouring whatever came to hand, in Yiddish, Russian, and even German, without my being truly proficient in any of them. Some of them were books in my uncle and aunt's library – classical pre-war works in Yiddish and German; others, newly published books from the Soviet Union, printed in hundreds of thousands of copies in Russian during the war years. The main subject of the latter was the heroic deeds of the Red Army in the battles to repel the invading armies on various fronts. Accompanying these tales were descriptions of the partisans' courageous acts as they fought in the rear against the invaders and of the way some captured partisans had been brutally executed by the Germans. Although the partisans had known that they were endangering their lives, they were determined to carry through with the weighty role that history – Soviet and universal – had imposed on them. Added to these were descriptions of the deep suffering that all strata of the Soviet population had gone through in its tremendous effort to reinforce the rear and the front where Red Army soldiers had fought from the beginning of the war until the defeat of Nazi Germany. My most beloved writer, whose stories captured my heart and who integrated all these elements into her stories, was Wanda Vasilevska, particularly in the book *Simply, Love.* The majority of films screened in the cinemas dealt with topics of war and heroism – some of them were documentary films intended, assumedly, to strengthen the spirit of the people and to deepen their patriotic consciousness in order to mobilize all the physical and spiritual forces of Soviet society to defeat the enemy.

We, who had returned from Transnistria, continued to live the events of the war. Not only did we update ourselves when watching the films about those chapters of war history that we had known nothing about, but I also felt a sense of revenge whenever seeing the German defeat.

In all these stories of heroism and suffering, no mention was made of the mass killing of Jews simply because they had been Jews in all the occupied territories of the Soviet Union and East European countries. Actually, for a long time we were unaware of the dimensions of the Holocaust under Nazi occupation. Only a long time afterwards did we learn of the extermination camps of Auschwitz, Treblinka, Birkenau, and Dachau.

As a result of our meeting, within the circle of our friends and acquaintances, survivors of Transnistria, we continued –

as we had a year earlier in Edinitz – to live the implications of the Holocaust. No wonder, then, that my rehabilitation process was remarkably slow. The burden of memories was too heavy, the horror stories of what had happened to our relatives, friends, and acquaintances who had perished during the Holocaust of the Jews of Bessarabia and Bucovina continued to echo in our minds, even if daily existence compelled us to integrate as quickly as possible into all spheres of normal life.

6 Breaking Through Barriers

My mother, my uncle, my aunts, my grandmother, and I – 15 years old – yearned for full rehabilitation, which seemed possible to us only in Eretz Israel. We no longer wanted to live among non-Jews who had taken an active role in the mass killings of Jews in Bessarabia and North Bucovina. Our goal was to live among our own people in the land of our forefathers, hoping that there we would be able to fulfil our national aspirations. This seemed quite attainable to us, if only we could cross the border to Romania – liberated and free – and from there embark on a ship sailing through the Black Sea to Eretz Israel. Everything seemed so simple. At that time I did not realize that our route to Eretz Israel would be very long, a journey lasting over a year. But even if we had known beforehand all that was going to happen to us, I doubt that anything would have deterred us from choosing this course.

We were not the only ones who thought this way. First, there were the Czernowitz Jews themselves, including the survivors who had returned from Transnistria, and, second, the many hundreds of refugees from all over Bessarabia who had gathered in the city. They, too, hoped and believed that from Czernowitz many would be able to cross the Soviet–Romanian border and from there continue on to Eretz Israel or America, even though the Soviet boundaries were closed for emigration. Their hope was based on the Soviet–Romanian repatriation agreement, which permitted Romanian citizens – refugees and prisoners – to return to Romania on the condition that they could prove they had been residents of Czernowitz before the outbreak of the war. Permission was granted in two stages: in April 1945 and

March 1946. Many who were not included in the defined category managed to obtain fictitious certificates meeting the requirements.

We were lucky, since all our family members were qualified for repatriation. When the border was reopened in March 1946 for return to Romania, our family did not hesitate about seizing this opportunity to 'escape'. Of course, our aim was not to settle in Romania but to use it as a way station towards emigration to Eretz Israel. We knew we would never realize our dream from the territory of the Soviet Union, since its borders to the west were hermetically sealed. As soon as we received the permit allowing us to pass over into Romania, we packed our meagre belongings and made our way to the crossing point to leave Soviet territory and enter Romania.

We said goodbye to my aunt Batia, who preferred to stay in Czernowitz, hoping for the return of her husband, Jacob Sinnreich, who had been mustered into the Red Army soon after war broke out. Separation from her was very difficult. After all we had made our way together to Transnistria and survived there thanks to mutual devotion, let alone mutual sacrifice, that characterized so much of our relationship. Twelve years would pass before we were reunited with her in Israel.

I bade farewell to Czernowitz with mixed emotions. I had loved this town from my early childhood. I liked its beautiful buildings of Austrian architectural style, the *Volksgarten* (Public Garden), outstanding for its flora among which I often used to walk, finding a bench to seclude myself and sit deeply absorbed in reading a book. I also loved my Yiddish state school, where I began the seventh grade (without completing it owing to our departure for Romania) taught by Jewish teachers. It was in this school that I first became fascinated with chemistry, so much so that I was sure that 'When I grow up, I shall be a chemist.' And I loved the Jewish State Theatre for its classical Jewish plays and for performances focusing on current themes. All this I had to leave behind without knowing exactly where I was going or to where my destiny would take me.

We travelled to the border, where hundreds of people were waiting their turn to pass over. We crossed it legally within the short time limit set by the Soviet authorities. So it was that we found ourselves one fine day on the other side of the border in the kingdom of Romania. The kingdom had revolted against Antonescu's Fascist regime on 23 August 1944 under the rule of King Mihai, with the help of the parties opposing Antonescu's government, and soon allied itself with the Soviet Union in its war against Nazi Germany.

During the summer of 1946 Romania was considered a free country. War criminals – amongst them Antonescu – were put on trial in a Romanian court; Antonescu and his close collaborators were sentenced to death, while other criminals received life sentences. (This trial took place before the Nuremberg trials of Nazi war criminals.)

Trade blossomed. Political parties operated freely, including the Zionist Organization. Freedom was palpable everywhere. Romania prepared itself for the elections held towards the end of 1946 that resulted in the triumph of the Communist Party and the removal of King Mihai from his throne even though he had been decorated with the most distinguished Soviet order – 'Hero of the Soviet Union' – for his part in the revolt against Antonescu and Nazi Germany.

After crossing the frontier, our first stop in Romania was in the South Bucovina town Siret because of its proximity to the Romanian–Soviet border. We stayed there for a short period of time. We were a group of some 40 people, including members of our family[41] and friends with whom we had passed over the border. This group of people sent a delegation, composed of my mother and two other members of the group, to the Zionist Organization in Bucharest to ask for its advice and guidance as to what arrangements should be made towards our immigration to Eretz Israel. A week later the delegation returned to Siret and following its advice, the whole group of forty took the train in the direction of Bucharest. Upon our arrival in Bucharest, the Zionist Organization placed us temporarily on a 'Hachshara' (preparation for *aliyah*) farm that it owned on the shore of Floriasca Lake. In a short time my mother joined in the teaching of Hebrew within the framework of Hechalutz, while I was sent to a summer camp not far from Sinaia. I spent almost two months there until my mother succeeded, by dint of great effort, to obtain – from the Eretz Israel emissaries in Bucharest responsible for *aliyah* – authorization for both of us to embark illegally on a refugee ship destined for Eretz Israel.

Once when I was waiting in line with my mother, together with many other people, to call upon the Eretz Israel emissary in charge of *aliyah* matters, I thought to myself, 'When I grow up, I will try to be an Eretz Israel emissary.' The idea of an emissary's mission fascinated me, the idea of being sent to redeem all of us and see us safely to the shores of Eretz Israel. This emissary, who daily received hundreds of people who had stood in line for hours hoping to obtain his authorization for *aliyah*, was none other than Shaike Dan,[42] who had parachuted onto Romanian soil in 1944 towards the final stage of the Second World War, shortly before the anti-Fascist revolt in Romania, aiming to assist members of the Jewish community in Romania to emigrate to Eretz Israel. From then until the last years of his life, he worked with utmost devotion and all his might for the cause of *aliyah* from the East European communist countries. He was able to do this as the person in charge, on behalf of the State of Israel, of the negotiations with representatives of the Romanian authorities, during the communist regime, on *aliyah* quotas to Israel as well as responsible for all aspects of effecting *aliyah*.[43] Over the course of time I worked in close cooperation with him when I directed the East European Department of Israel's Ministry of Foreign Affairs in Jerusalem and later on when I served as Israel's ambassador to Romania.

7 Illegal Immigration: The Long Way Home to Eretz Israel

On 13 September 1946, my mother and I, together with over 3,000 others, left Bucharest by train in the direction of the Romania–Yugoslavia border. The train passed through breathtaking landscapes. I was in high spirits; these were the happiest moments in our life. Two diasporas and one hell were behind us. Finally, ahead of us lay the way to Eretz Israel, the road to our future. I thanked the Almighty for having brought us to this stage, praying for our safe arrival in Eretz Israel, once again with His help.

Some youngsters, myself included, sang songs all along the way. The songs were mainly from the Russia repertoire and partly from the pool of Yiddish and Hebrew ones. We were lifting our voices to express the happiness that filled our hearts. As soon as we crossed the Yugoslav border, we found out that the way to Eretz Israel was not as short as it had seemed to us, nor was it paved with roses.

In Yugoslavia we were transferred, through Belgrade, to Zagreb. We were placed in a long, empty, multi-storeyed building, apparently in its final stages of construction, located outside the city. We were told that it belonged to the Maximir University of Zagreb and was destined to become a hospital. It had no windows or doors yet,and was wide open on every side. Each of us was assigned a small part of the floor large enough to sleep on. We were supposed to stay there only a few days until we embarked for Eretz Israel, but those days turned into six weeks. Presumably, the ship was not ready to take us all on board. Floors had to be constructed in its inner space to make room for all the refugees. Another ship that was supposed to sail with ours had not yet arrived in the little fishing port from which we were about to depart.

Owing to the overcrowding in the building and the absence of proper sanitation, infectious diseases broke out among the refugees. Fortunately, there were physicians among us who could provide medical aid to anyone in need, and there was no lack of medicines. Every morning people waited in long lines for an appointment with the doctors. In addition to disease, we had to face a severely cold winter, with the whole wide-open building exposed to winds and rain. The emissaries of the Aliyah Bet (Illegal Immigration to Eretz Israel) Department, who had accompanied the refugees to Yugoslavia – among them Shaike Dan – found a way to transfer the women, the children, and the elderly to shacks in town, where they would stay until our ship was ready for boarding.

Only at the beginning of November 1946 did our redemption come. We left Zagreb by train, arriving at a small fishing port, Bakar, on the Adriatic shore. My mother and I were sent to the large ship that took on 3,000 refugees, while about 500 refugees were taken to the smaller ship. We were assigned to one of the ship's eight floors that were arranged in the form of pallets next to a stepladder that ran from the bottom to the top of the ship. The distance between one pallet and the next was about 30 cm. People could only lie down on their allotted space, one next to the other, with practically no space between them. Later on I read that this ship, first called *Tnu'at ha-Meri* (Rebellion Movement) and then *Knesset Israel*, could hold, according to its weight and capacity, some 350 people: the number it took on was ten times more.

We were allowed to step on to the deck only in small groups so that the British Air Force would not discover our presence. Once on deck there was a great deal of seasickness, since the passengers had no experience of sea travel. On top of that the sea was stormy and a great deal of vomiting ensued, which was difficult to bear. As a result the travellers preferred to be packed between the eight floors rather than climbing up to the deck for fresh air. Food (basically canned goods) and water were rationed to make sure the amount on hand would last for the voyage of 10 to 14 days.

Several days after setting sail from Bakar, we ran into tempestuous storms. Our ship dipped from side to side, and the passengers swayed along with it. Hidden fears and deep despair gripped all of us. One night, with almost certain death awaiting us, the shipped anchored at sea. Perhaps that prevented its sinking. No one could remain on deck for any time at all, since huge waves constantly swept over it. It was obvious that anyone who would try to stand there would immediately be washed away. To escape the claws of death in Transnistria only to drown afterwards in the sea on way to Eretz Israel, the goal so fervently wished for, seemed to me to be the greatest absurdity.

And how did the commanders of the ship assess the situation? In Yossi Harel's testimony, which I read much later on, he says, among other things:

> In one of the big storms the ship was carried by the waves and was about to sink … All our attempts to turn the ship around were useless. The weak engine was powerless in the face of the turbulent waves. The anticipated disaster seemed very near … The storm we had been caught up in … was seen even by those who know nothing about seamanship as the approaching end of their fate. Only a sudden change in the direction of the wind, and with it a change in the direction of the waves, saved the lives of the refugees from a certain death.[43]

A few days before the big storm we were informed that the small ship called *Abba Berditchev*[44] which was accompanying the *Knesset Israel*, was going to sink at any moment – the ship could not withstand the wild waves battering it. The resourcefulness of our emissaries – the commanders of both ships, Benjamin Yerushalmi and Yossi Harel – plus the help of the

Greek captain rescued all the refugees on the *Abba Berditchev* by transferring them in time to lifeboats and setting them down on a rocky shore. No one was injured. Then, with the assistance of Yugoslav fisherman and policemen, all the refugees boarded Yugoslav boats and were brought to our ship, *Knesset Israel,* while watching the *Abba Berditchev* sink. This was a miracle from heaven. But it was also the drama we saw in our mind's eye when the huge storm threatened to split our overweight ship – this was the source of our fear and despair. The number of refugees on our ship now reached 3,845, the largest number of 'illegal' refugees to that date on an 'illegal' ship bound for the 'safe shores of Eretz Israel'.

When the sea calmed down and the anchor raised, the ship sailed once again, making its slow but steady way towards our goal – again we saw this as a miracle from heaven. The Mediterranean was quite calm when we entered it, reinforcing our hope of safely reaching the shores of our historic homeland. Unfortunately, on 24 November 1946 our ship was spotted by British military aircraft and the following day, three British destroyers came alongside us. From that moment on they were a constant presence. Our voyage, which was supposed to last seven to ten days, actually took 23 days. Not only did the severe storms we encountered at sea delay us, but also the excess weight the boat was carrying forced the captain to slow our pace.

On 26 November 1946 the *Knesset Israel* reached the port of Haifa. Troops of the British Royal Navy immediately began to climb aboard with the purpose of transferring all the passengers to the destroyers. A big surprise awaited them. The refugees opposed them with all their might. They heaved canned goods and pieces of wood at the British soldiers and threw them off the ladders the British had put up on the sides of the ship to climb to the deck. They also grappled with the soldiers who had made it to the deck to drag the refugees by force to the destroyers. In response to the strong, unexpected resistance – an unprecedented situation on illegal refugee ships, according to Yossi Harel's testimony – the British soldiers fired at the refugees near them. Two refugees were killed on the spot, one of them a 17-year-old; many others were wounded. What a sorry tragedy – to survive the Nazi death camps, to reach the shores of Eretz Israel and be killed so close to them by the bullet of a British soldier! The refugees' strong resistance almost totally collapsed when the British threw tear gas bombs towards us, on the deck as well as into the innards of the ship where the majority of refugees huddled. The gas bombs forced them all to climb up to the deck with their last bit of strength to breathe fresh air. The more we rubbed our eyes, the more they stung, and we could not see a thing. This was our first experience with tear gas. But the most painful thing was that we were to be forced away from our historic homeland, the goal of our aspirations from the time we had our first inklings of consciousness of self – particularly after we had succeeded in escaping the inferno of Transnistria and two diasporas.

We were roughly transferred to the British ships that stood in place for three days. I shall never forget the view of Mount Carmel that was opposite us, nor that of Haifa during the daytime and its lights at night. Everything seemed so near, and yet so far away.

At a later stage, we learned that the resistance of the *Knesset Israel* refugees against the British Navy reverberated strongly in the Eretz Israel press.[45] The editorials strongly called for the British authorities to permit the refugees to remain in the country. The Jewish population held a large demonstration in the streets of Haifa as an act of solidarity with the refugees' struggle and their demand to stay in Eretz Israel. Moreover, in Jerusalem an application was submitted for a habeas corpus to the British Supreme Court on behalf of Jerusalem's Jewish community committee through the lawyers I. D. Goitein and A. Spaer against seven government authorities (the chief commander of the British Army in Palestine, the military commander of Haifa, the director-general of the police force, the commander of Haifa Port, and the captains of the three British destroyers) requesting them to substantiate why they would not prevent the expulsion of the *Knesset Israel* refugees from their country, Eretz Israel, considering it an illegal act. In response the Supreme Court issued an order to delay the expulsion of the refugees. As long as the status of the application had not been clarified in court, the British destroyers were not permitted to leave the shores of the country. The petition was reviewed in the Supreme Court, which rejected it and ruled that the expulsion order was based on Para. 112 of the Defence Regulations (Emergency) Act 1945 and had been issued according to the authority of the high commissioner in cases such as this one.[46] So it was that we were transported, against our will, on 30 November 1946, by the three British destroyers to the deportation island of Cyprus.

The Jewish Agency for Palestine and the directors of the National Committee of the Yishuv (Jewish community) published the following statement on 2 December 1946:

> The expulsion from the country of 4,000 Jewish refugees who arrived last week on the ship *Knesset Israel* produced grief and bitterness in the Yishuv and amongst the Jewish people all over the world. The Jewish Agency and the Va'ad Le'umi [National Committee] submitted an urgent petition to the Government demanding the cessation of expulsions that cause only additional suffering to the survivors of the Nazi Holocaust, and in this case, also caused bloodshed. As experience has shown, these expulsions are powerless from preventing anyone desirous of life from taking the danger-fraught road. We most certainly hoped that these petitions and the understanding of the deep distress these expulsions create in all circles of the Yishuv would propel the Government into ceasing from acting in this tragic manner. Unfortunately our hopes were dashed ... Our firm aim is to correct the situation and lead to [better] understanding in Eretz Israel. But the Yishuv, the Zionist movement, and the entire Jewish people will not rest nor hold its peace as long as the gates to the country will not be open

> for Jewish immigration (*aliyah*) to it and absorption in it by right and with dignity.[47]

As we made our way to Cyprus we did not know about any of this. We learned of it only after we were imprisoned behind the barbed wire of the refugee camps. The Yishuv reaction sounded to us like the strongest ever heard in comparison to the responses to the expulsion to Cyprus of previous refugee ships. Moreover, the claim submitted to the Supreme Court was the first of its kind and compelled the British authorities to also contend with the refugees on the judicial level, meaning that no one should be expelled from the country before being detained and before a court hearing of the case.

Looking back, we can see that the struggle of the *Knesset Israel* refugees and their expulsion to Cyprus served the cause of the refugees themselves, since they no longer felt they were alone in the world and knew that the Yishuv in the country stood behind them and continued to act on their behalf. They had proved to themselves that they were capable of standing up to the Imperial British soldiers by power of their moral stance, without arms in hand. This was a battle of 'no choice', perhaps even before this concept became known during Israel's War of Independence. The refugees' struggle and their expulsion to Cyprus also served the cause of the Yishuv in Eretz Israel in its vigorous demand to open the country's gates to Holocaust survivors. It also helped considerably in arousing enlightened world public opinion (which had done little to save European Jews under the Nazi occupation) and in carrying on with the determined Zionist struggle in the international arena from a position of moral strength. So it was that the struggle of the illegal refugees became an integral part of the general national and Zionist battle that led to the bringing of the Palestine question before the United Nations organizations and subsequently to the establishment of the State of Israel.

8 In the British Detention Camps of Cyprus and Atlit

On 1 December 1946, two days after we were expelled from the Eretz Israel shores together with all the other *Knesset Israel* refugees – except for several dozens of Jews who had been wounded during the struggle with the British fleet officers and brought down on stretchers for medical treatment at Haifa hospitals – the three British destroyers carrying the refugees anchored in the Cyprus port of Famagusta. As we were taken down to the shore British soldiers completely surrounded us. They guarded us tightly, apparently for fear that one of us would escape.

From the top of a hill young Cypriots threw several copies of the Cyprus English newspaper Cyprus Mail towards us; the paper told of the expulsion of the 3,800 refugees on the *Knesset Israel* to detention camps in Cyprus. I did not know English at that time, but those of us who understood it well found a sympathetic description of us in the issue. By tossing the papers the local youth demonstrated solidarity with us, much to the consternation of the British, over our being brought by force by the British Empire to their island, then under British rule. At the shore the British soldiers loaded us onto trucks that took us to a detention camp where hundreds of tents had been erected on a large area enclosed with barbed wire.

The first thought that crossed my mind – and I assume the minds of many other *Knesset Israel* refugees, the majority of whom were Holocaust survivors – was a comparison between the ghettos of Transnistria and the detention camp to which we had be taken. Neither I nor anyone else had imagined that, two and a half years after our liberation by the Red Army in Transnistria and about a year and a half after the victory of the

Allied Forces over Nazi Germany, we would be held once again as prisoners and interned in detention camps behind barbed wire for our single sin of wanting to emigrate to the land of our forefathers.

This was my first acquaintance with 'Summer Camp' No. 63 in Karaolos. We were led to tents, housing about twelve people each, with beds and blankets for everyone. The weather was wintry and rainy. The ground between the tents was muddy. The personal belongings of all the refugees were thrown onto an open site. Much effort was needed to identify our own luggage, packed mainly in knapsacks that were wet through with rain and dirty because of the mud. This was the only property we had carried before embarking on the *Knesset Israel*. The camp authorities distributed to all of us, through the camp's Refugee Committee, foodstuffs called 'products', without ever entering the camp themselves. So we became prisoners of a special kind. Sitting in the tents was quite depressing. We could hardly sleep, despite being exhausted from our long sea journey and our struggle to be permitted to enter Eretz Israel. But above all, we were concerned about the future. How long we would have to live under such conditions?

During our first days in the camp great chaos reigned. It became obvious that the British authorities were unprepared to absorb such a large number of people in this camp, and since there was significant overcrowding the authorities decided to transfer a large part of the *Knesset Israel* refugees – particularly children and their parents, as well as individual youngsters – to 'Winter Camp' No. 64 in Dekilia, where hundreds of sheet-metal huts had been erected on a vast area. My mother and I, as well as the majority of other *Knesset Israel* refugees, were included amongst those scheduled for transfer to the 'Winter Camp' shortly after our imprisonment in the 'Summer Camp'.

At first, life in this camp was more bearable than in the 'Summer Camp'. Each hut was divided into two living units with a separate entrance. Four or five people (or two families) were placed in each unit. The roof was round – cold in winter, hot in summer – and the floor was cement. Public showers and lavatories were also installed separately in the same type of huts, as were the public kitchen, the clinic, and the infant centre. At a later stage schools, libraries, and reading rooms were opened in similar structures. High barbed-wire fences ringed the camp. Every 20–30 metres stood a watchtower. All night long, from these positions, sentinels lit up the barbed wire to prevent detainees from escaping in the dark. The camp's entrance gate was high and locked. Nobody could pass through without permission. Camp headquarters were outside but close to the gate, across the barbed wire. The refugees' representatives used to conduct talks on the organizational life in the camp with the camp commander in the headquarters' offices.

We were not the first refugees to be taken to these camps. After we had been in the camp for a few days we learned that in our vicinity there were other camps that had been established a few months earlier where refugees taken from previous ships had already been interned. News about banning refugees on illegal ships to Cyprus had reached us, mainly through the communications media, before our departure from Bucharest. What we had not known then, and what we learned only after expulsion to Cyprus, was the number of refugees anticipating aliyah to Eretz Israel who ended up in Cyprus awaiting an aliyah certificate granted at the rate of only 750 a month for Cyprus detainees. The same quota was allotted for displaced persons in Europe on the basis of 'first to arrive, first to leave'. With *Knesset Israel* refugees detained in Cyprus numbering some 3,800, it was necessary to hold a lottery each month among them to determine the lucky winners of the 750 certificates. It would take about five months for all *Knesset Israel* refugees to obtain the desired certificate – but their time would not come until all previous Cyprus detainees had received permission to enter Eretz Israel. The approximate date for our first drawing was June 1947. Calculating from this we could tell that the immigration to Eretz Israel of the *Knesset Israel* refugees would take place between eight to twelve months after their detention in Cyprus. This was a very sad forecast, making necessary long-term organization in the detention camps. Our names – my mother's and mine – came up only in the fourth round of drawings, so we were destined to eleven months of detention in the camp, from the beginning of December 1946 until mid-October 1947.

The comparison I made upon our arrival in the Cyprus detention camps between them and the Transnistria ghettos was unjust. In two aspects it was apt: the detention of refugees surrounded by barbed wire and the negation of their freedom. All other domains of camp life differed from ghetto life.

First, there was no physical threat to our existence. We knew this was a transitory stage as well as the final one on our road to legal *aliyah* to Eretz Israel, even if, in our specific case, as it became clear to us, the 'waiting list' was much longer than we had anticipated.

Second, we were allowed to correspond freely with relatives abroad and to receive material aid from them to help overcome our shortages. The Hebrew press that we received regularly helped us follow current events in Eretz Israel closely. This included the united struggle of the Yishuv leadership to gain permission for free immigration to Eretz Israel and to establish an independent Jewish state in the territory of Palestine. We did not feel isolated, lonely, or forgotten, as this encouraged us greatly and gave us the fortitude to withstand the period of detention.

Third, the British authorities provided us with food sufficient for our daily needs, while the American Jewish Joint Distribution Committee (the Joint) supplied us with clothing, health services, and education.

Fourth, in addition to the clinic and the babies' home in our camp, No. 64 (as well as in the other camps), operated by a team of physicians and nurses from among the refugees and emissaries from Eretz Israel, the British authorities offered medical assistance to all in need at a British hospital in Nicosia, particularly to women who were about to give birth.

Fifth, the self-organization in the camp operated without intervention, either direct nor indirect, from the British camp headquarters. Each camp had its own secretariat composed of representatives of the Zionist movements active in the camps (in addition to a common secretariat of all the camps), which dealt with organizing internal life in the camp and conducted negotiations with the camp headquarters whenever necessary.

Sixth, we received educational assistance from the Jewish Agency in Jerusalem and from Youth Aliyah as well as hundreds of books from The Committee for the Deportees in Cyprus (founded in Eretz Israel by the national institutions in early 1947). They helped in the operation of an educational and cultural system that was a most important tool for helping youngsters and adults in the study of the Hebrew language and the completion of their general and Jewish education; which had been denied them during the Holocaust years. At first, the teachers came from among the refugees; the staff was later reinforced by the arrival of teaching emissaries from Eretz Israel who worked in the camps until their closure.

All the teachers devoted themselves wholeheartedly to the educational tasks, including adult courses for Hebrew study, be it in the 'youth village' established in 1947 in Camp No. 65 or in the schools that functioned as part of the activities of the various Zionist movements, such as in Camp No. 64. The teachers helped suffuse the atmosphere around us with Eretz Israel: it penetrated it into our very being and giving us the feeling that 'Cyprus is also Eretz Israel'. (This was the title of a song we sang in the detention camps; it was based on a Russian song, 'Siberia is also Russian soil'.) Thanks to these teachers and the Eretz Israel atmosphere in which we were steeped in our daily lives, the refugees were well trained for their quick absorption in Israel in all spheres: from taking part in the battles in Israel's War of Independence (where many immigrants fell at the fronts) and joining kibbutzim (communal settlements) and moshavim (cooperative settlements) to carrying out various functions in the fields of security, medicine, engineering, law, trade, economy, industry, agriculture, education, culture, diplomatic service, and public administration, as well as participating actively in political and ideological parties, the General Labour Federation, and research and educational institutions.

How did we, my mother and I, integrate into the camp's daily life?

Soon after we were transferred to Camp No. 64, communal organization began functioning there. One of the primary needs was to set up schools for the youth and courses for teaching adults Hebrew. My mother was among the founders of the Ichud (Unity) School for children whose parents belonged to the Mapai Party (the Workers of Eretz Israel Party). Simultaneously, other schools were opened as part of party activities, and they, too, were operated with the help of teachers from amongst the refugees. (The 'youth village' that became famous in Camp No. 65 spent its initial stages in Camp No. 64. At the outset the village was operated by refugee teachers; only later on was the village helped by teacher-emissaries from Eretz Israel.) More than 100 pupils, aged 7 to 16, studied at the Ichud School. My mother taught several classes a day, about 5 hours every morning: Hebrew language and literature, Bible, and geography of Eretz Israel. Until textbooks were received – from 'The Committee for the Deportees in Cyprus' – my mother taught without books or teaching aids. In the early afternoon my mother taught two youngsters my age together with me, mainly Hebrew grammar and Bible. Though the three of us had some basis for these subjects, her job was not easy. In the late afternoon hours my mother gave Hebrew language courses for adults, one for beginners, the other for advanced. She devoted herself wholeheartedly to pedagogical activity with the idealistic enthusiasm that was characteristic of many others of her generation, the generation of pioneers. She was involved non-stop in education during our entire stay in Camp No. 64 – except for Saturdays and holidays for which she prepared her pupils in accordance with the best of Jewish national tradition. All of this was, of course, done without any payment or material benefit. The teacher-emissaries who were active in the 'Youth Village' – among them Dr. Hanoch Reinhold (later Rinot) – were more than surprised when they came to know her pedagogical achievements and her vast knowledge of Hebrew subjects.

It would not be wrong for me to say that my mother saw this period of teaching Hebrew to young people and adults and making real to them the atmosphere of Eretz Israel life – even though she had never been there – as her busiest time and the one with the greatest achievements in all her history of pedagogical activity in the Diaspora and later in Israel. After their immigration to Israel, many of her pupils kept in close contact with her. Under her influence some of them trained as teachers, thus becoming her colleagues. More than once I heard from them that the memory of that period in Cyprus would be cherished by them forever.

I found a place for myself in the studies and immersed myself in reading books. In the camp a very rich library, containing the best works in Hebrew and general literature, was set up with the assistance of the Youth and Hechalutz Department of the World Zionist Organization and the Committee for the Deportees in Cyprus. I swallowed every book I came across. My hunger to broaden my horizons was insatiable. The lessons I received from my mother had, of course, helped me understand the content of the books, the majority of which I read in Hebrew.

When a seminar, founded by 'Beit Hanoar Rutenberg' on Mount Carmel in Haifa, opened in our camp for training instructors I submitted my candidacy. There was more than a pinch of impudence in this act, since older people than I, with greater formal education than I had, and with some experience in teaching (while I had none), also applied to the seminar. Selection was very strict and not all candidates were accepted. I remember myself sitting all excited opposite the teacher-emissary Baruch Rubinstein, the person behind the establishment of this seminar, answering his questions, related mainly to knowledge of Hebrew and general education. I was probably among the minority who responded to the question 'What is your education?' with 'seven grades in a Soviet state school in Czernowitz' (which I really did not finish because of our departure from the Soviet Union on our way to Eretz Israel). I felt – and perhaps my examiners thought so, too – that were I accepted to the seminar it would be as if I had jumped from public school directly to university, without any proper prior training.

To my joy and surprise I was accepted. Studies lasted two months, six hours a day in the classroom, six hours a day doing homework and reading the required bibliography. I doubt whether I ever enjoyed studying as much as when I was at the seminar, subjects including Hebrew literature, Bible, history of the Jewish people, history of Zionism, and learning about Eretz Israel. We also had lectures on psychology and sociology. Every teacher and lecturer excited us. We took in every word they uttered. For the first time in our lives we were gaining knowledge from Eretz Israel teachers, in Hebrew, in an Eretz Israel atmosphere following an Eretz Israel curriculum. They set before us the whole realm of knowledge. In addition to Baruch Rubinstein, the team of teachers included Shmuel Werses (later a Hebrew University professor of Hebrew Literature), Shmaryahu Zalmanovitch (later Sh. Talmon, a Hebrew University professor of Bible), Emanuel Nadav (who fell in the Old City during the siege of Jerusalem), who used to sit with us, his students, and teach us Eretz Israel songs as if he were one of us, a modest, noble person with many plans for the future, and Israel Moshe Horn (who fell in the defence of Jerusalem), who had a vast knowledge of world culture. Another figure I remember well is the Jerusalem teacher Ben-Menachem, a superb lecturer on Hebrew literature.

The seminar produced many graduates; it continued to operate in the Cyprus refugees camps until they were closed. It was an extraordinary educational-cultural enterprise of great significance. I am confident that its alumni (some of whom studied with me at the Hebrew university of Jerusalem in the mid-1950s), wherever they may be, seriously appreciated and admired it as an important landmark in their lives.

When looking back today on the detention period in Cyprus, I cannot but note that it was a 'blessing of the curse'. Though we lived behind barbed wire, we benefited significantly from our stay in the camp – in the process of 'returning to ourselves', developing our personalities, acquiring self-confidence, and training well towards our future in Israel. All this in addition to closing, to a certain extent, the gap in our education that had opened during that terrible period in our lives in the shadow of destruction.

About two weeks before our release from the Cyprus detention camp, our close relatives arrived there. We had been separated from them since our departure from Bucharest. The group included my grandmother Lea Lerner, my uncle Yosef, his wife Hanna, and their son Jacob as well as my aunt Shoshana Lerner. They had sailed illegally on the *Geula* that traveled together with the ship *Medinat ha-Yehudim*, from a Bulgarian port and were interned in the Cyprus refugee summer camp for about eight months before proceeding to Israel. During their detention, my uncle Yosef and my aunt Shoshana gave Hebrew lessons to youths and adults. Both my aunt and uncle had previous experience in teaching Hebrew, and they continued with their educational activity the entire time they were in Cyprus, teaching the language and Hebrew literature to dozens of refugees to prepare them for emigration to Israel.

We were transferred from Cyprus to the Atlit detention camp where we stayed about two months. We arrived there six weeks before 29 November 1947, the day the UN General Assembly decided to recommend the partition of Palestine into two states, one Jewish, the other Arab. Overwhelming joy reigned in the Atlit camp as it did throughout the Yishuv. At a festive meeting in the camp on the occasion of this historic date, spokesmen of different parties addressed the public, made up entirely of refugees detained for a short transitory period. My mother was the prime spokesman for Mapai. She spoke (in Hebrew) about the significance of this UN resolution that would not have been accepted by the General Assembly had it not been for those who had laid the foundation of Jewish settlement in Eretz Israel and without the struggle of the Zionist leadership for free immigration and for the establishment of a Jewish state in Eretz Israel. She spotlighted the role of the Holocaust survivors and the waves of illegal immigration to Eretz Israel as factors that certainly influenced the passing of this historic resolution. In concluding she noted that the road to establishing our independence was still long and that each of us, whether in or out of the detention camps, had to lend a hand in achieving this supreme goal. Her speech was mentioned in a Hebrew newspaper that covered this event. I listened to her words with great admiration, seeing in her a symbol of our national revival. It was hard for me to differentiate between the refugee, survivor of Transnistria, and the Zionist activist in Eretz Israel.

We celebrated the Hanukkah festival in the Atlit camp. This was our first holiday on Eretz Israel soil. My mother prepared a performance with some of her pupils, who had been transferred with us to Atlit; the show earned great applause. To our joy, the Hanukkah festivities went on for hours. At the same time, it was difficult to free ourselves from the feeling of sadness pervasive in the camp in the wake of the first wave of Arab terror against the Jews. It had occurred the morning after the historic UN resolution of 29 November 1947 as an expression of the Arabs determined opposition to it.

*

Near the barbed wire next to the entrance gate to the camp, my aunt Sonia Lerner-Barles (my mother's sister) and her 3-year-old daughter Zipora came to meet us after a 12-year separation that included the Holocaust years. Both sisters were extremely excited, standing wordless opposite each other, with the barbed-wire fence in between. A British sentinel watched us, warning us after a short while that the five minutes allotted for such an 'interview' were over.

6. Myself, a year after the liberation, Czernowitz, 1945

7. My mother Zadcanit and myself in detention camp 64, Cyprus

8. My mother Zadcanit with her Ichud school class. In the background are the barbed-wire fence and the British military observation point

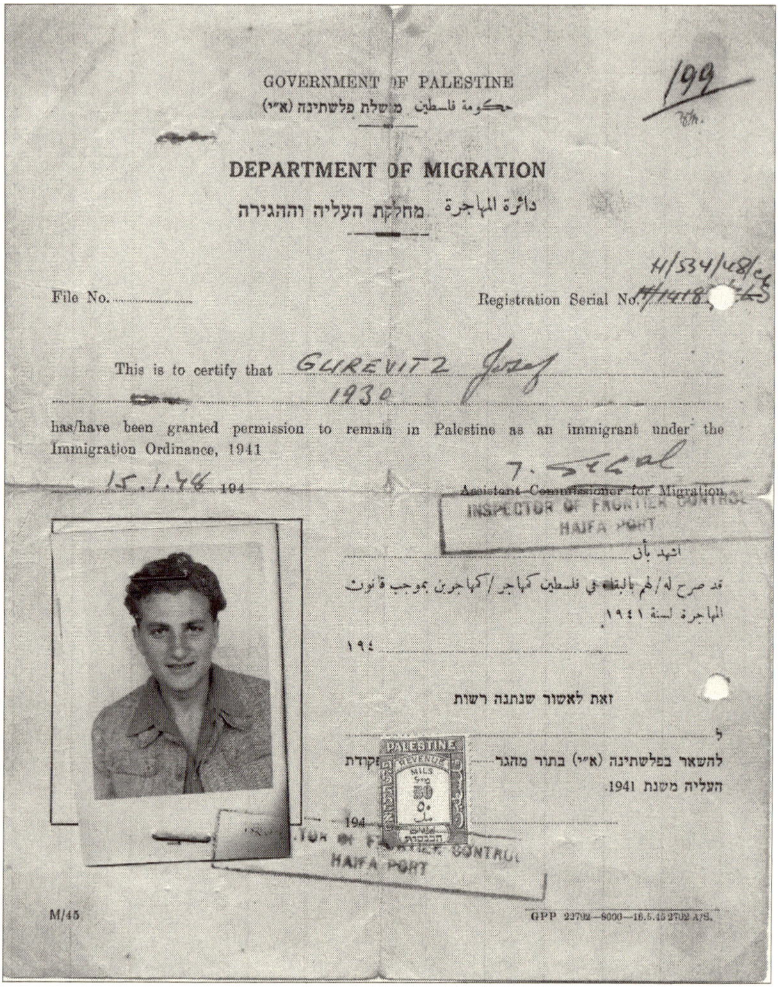
199

GOVERNMENT OF PALESTINE

حكومة فلسطين ממשלת פלשתינה (א״י)

DEPARTMENT OF MIGRATION

מחלקת העליה וההגירה دائرة المهاجرة

H/534/48/cc

File No. .... Registration Serial No. H/1418/...

This is to certify that GUREVITZ Josef

1930

has/have been granted permission to remain in Palestine as an immigrant under the Immigration Ordinance, 1941

15.1.48 194

J. Segal

Assistant Commissioner for Migration

INSPECTOR OF FRONTIER CONTROL HAIFA PORT

اشهد بان

قد صرح له/لهم بالبقاء في فلسطين كمهاجر/كمهاجرين بموجب قانون المهاجرة لسنة ١٩٤١

١٩٤

זאת לאשור שנתנה רשות

ל

להשאר בפלשתינה (א״י) בתור מהגר ... פקודת העליה משנת 1941.

194

PALESTINE REVENUE 50 MILS

INSPECTOR OF FRONTIER CONTROL HAIFA PORT

M/45

GPP 23702—8000—18.5.45 2702 A/S.

9. My permission for *aliyah* to Eretz Israel issued to me by the Department of Immigration of the Government of Palestine (Eretz Israel)

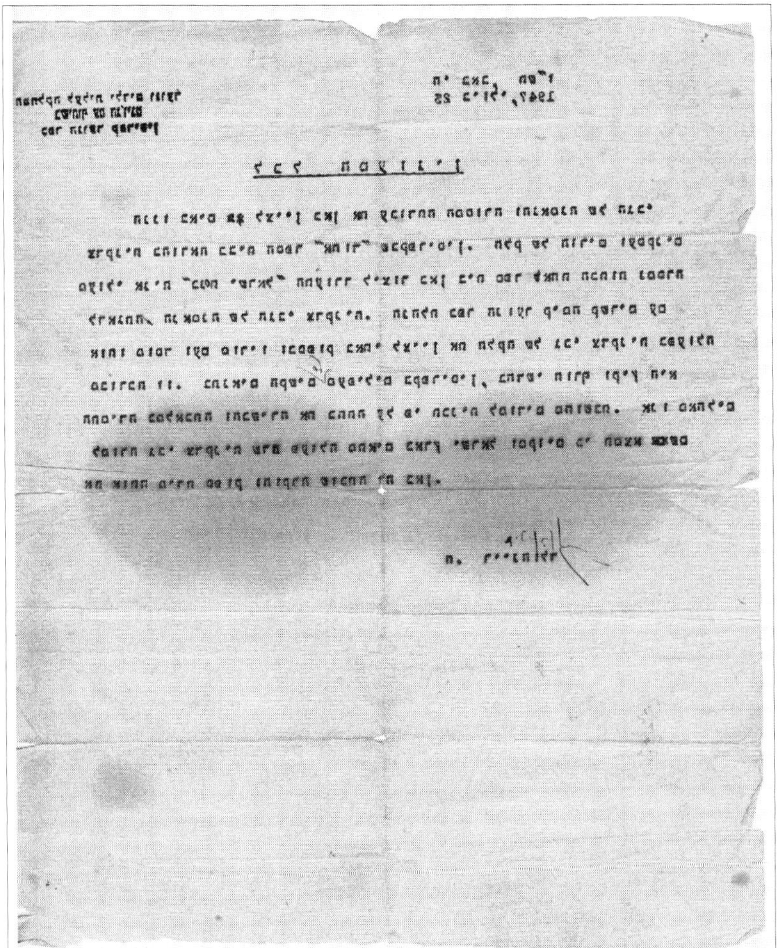

10. A letter of appreciation, dated 23 July 1947, presented to my mother Zadcanit on behalf of Youth Aliyah (of the Zionist Organization) before our *aliyah* to Eretz Israel, signed by Hanoch Reinhold (later Rinott, director general of Israel's Ministry of Education and Culture), who was the Youth Aliyah representative in the Cyprus detention camps

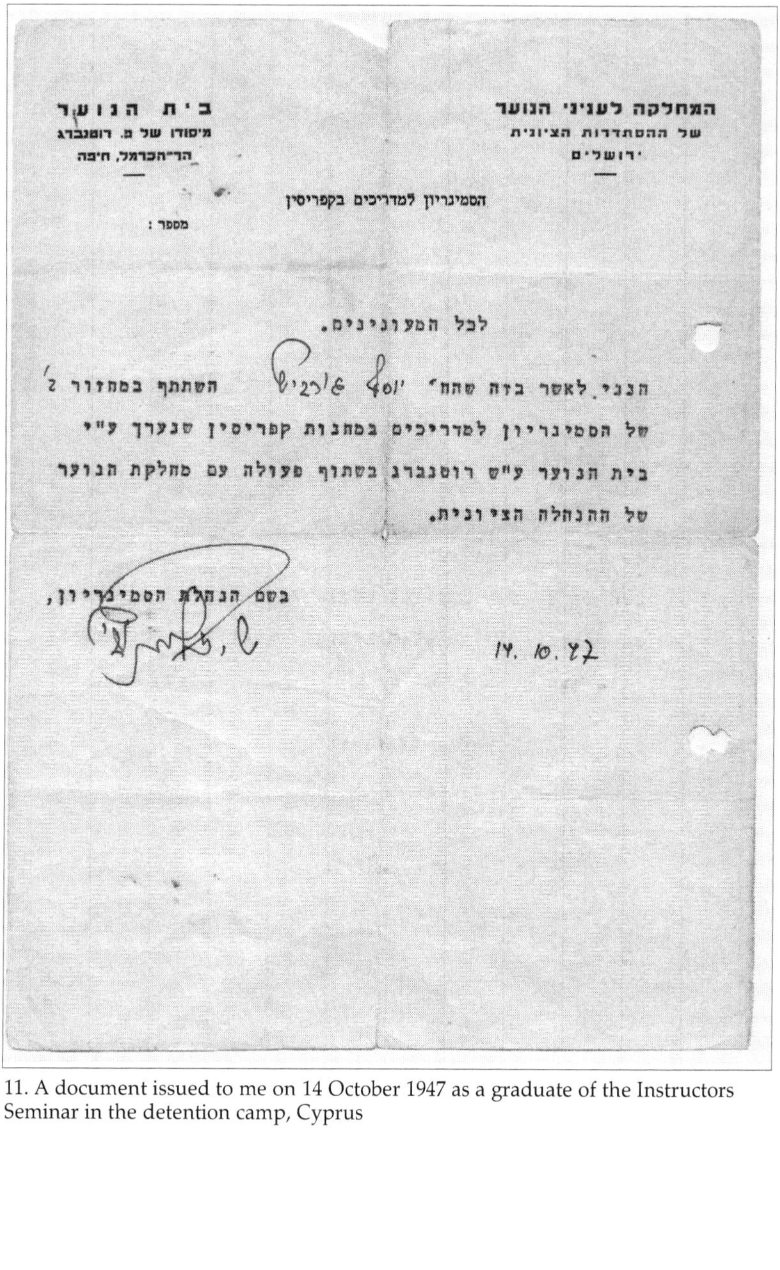

המחלקה לעניני הנוער
של ההסתדרות הציונית
ירושלים

בית הנוער
מיסודו של פ. רוטנברג
הר־הכרמל, חיפה

הסמינריון למדריכים בקפריסין

מספר :

לכל המעונינים.

הנני לאשר בזה שהח׳ יוסף אירגיש השתתף במחזור ז׳
של הסמינריון למדריכים במחנות קפריסין שנערך ע״י
בית הנוער ע״ש רוטנברג בשתוף פעולה עם מחלקת הנוער
של ההנהלה הציונית.

בשם הנהלת הסמינריון,

14.10.47

11. A document issued to me on 14 October 1947 as a graduate of the Instructors Seminar in the detention camp, Cyprus

9 Free in Eretz Israel

On 15 December 1947, my mother and I were released from the Atlit detention camp and 'granted permission to remain in Palestine (Eretz Israel) as immigrants under the Immigration Ordinance 1941'. This happened thirteen months after we had embarked on the *Knesset Israel* as illegal immigrants on our long way to Eretz Israel. We became, once again, free people, without knowing how to enjoy this freedom, how and where to settle down, how to integrate into daily life, and how to secure our future, starting as we were with no material basis.

The first thing we did was to take the bus leaving for Haifa, where my aunt Sonia, her husband Zeev Barles, and their daughter Zipora lived in a one-room apartment on Hechalutz Street. We did not have a penny to pay for our bus tickets. Fortunately, the bus driver, seeing that we were newcomers with small luggage in hand, was good enough to forgo the payment for the ride and even showed us where to get off near our relatives' building. This was our first trip in a passenger bus as free people, and I can never forget that we didn't even have the means to pay for it.

We stayed with our relatives for about a week. From there we moved to what was then known as 'Beit Olim' (immigrants' home) in Bat Galim near Haifa, owned and financed by the Jewish Agency. This was a kind of boarding house with many newcomers crowded in several rooms. Since my mother could not find a job as a teacher in Haifa at that time, we moved to Tel Aviv where chances to do so were much better. Our Beit Olim this time, on Aliya Street, operated under the same conditions as in Bat Galim. My mother was promised a job in the area and after a short while we left the immigrants' home, which had been most helpful when taking our first steps as free people in our own homeland; we were equipped with two metal beds (one under the other), two blankets that we received, like any other newcomer, from the Jewish Agency – and a heavy load of optimism. Thus we began our newly free, independent life in Eretz Israel.

Those were the last months of British rule in Palestine. Since 30 November 1947, one day after the UN resolution on the partition of Palestine, the Arab inhabitants of the country had perpetrated more and more terrorist acts. The result was an ever-increasing number of Jews wounded or murdered. The Yishuv had to defend itself in Galilee, the Negev, Jerusalem, and the centre of the country – with almost a total lack of military means, being dependent upon the British Police, which in most cases was either indifferent or indirectly supportive of the Arab attacks.

At the United Nations debates were waged on the country's future, and it seemed that the British Mandate on Palestine would not end on 15 May, but either be extended or taken over through some UN-approved arrangements.

Tension ran high. Nevertheless, the Yishuv made all possible preparations towards the end of the British Mandate, even militarily, but with very poor resources. The familiar slogan 'the whole country is a battlefield and the entire nation an army' became real.

And then, the voice of David Ben-Gurion rang out on 14 May 1948, declaring, at a festive meeting of the leaders of all political parties, the establishment of a Jewish state in Eretz Israel, called the State of Israel. The Arab population rebuffed this declaration by opening an armed attack on all Jewish settlements with the help of armies of seven Arab states that invaded the territory of Palestine. We were on the brink of our War of Independence. Here we were, facing another war, but this time of a different nature: defending our independent existence as a free state and nation. The heroic acts of the young fighters from the Yishuv deeply inspired our national cause and took on the status of myths. They imbued us with idealistic enthusiasm that immediately banished any remnant of fear and weakness from our past. Victory was finally ours, paid at the enormous price of the lives of young men and women who sacrificed themselves for our independent statehood. We were born again, the state and ourselves.

*

My mother soon re-entered the teaching profession, working in it continuously for 18 years, until her retirement because of ill-health. She was a teacher and educator for the fifth to eighth grades in Beit Hinuch school 'Neve Sha'anan' – later called the Vitkin School, a state school in Shekhunat Schapira, an old suburb of Tel Aviv, populated by families from different communities, including newcomers to the country. She was held in high regard as a teacher, not only by the various inspectors of the Ministry of Education and Culture, who sent teacher seminar students to her classes to observe her lessons as part of their training, but – and mainly – by her own pupils and their parents.

In addition to imparting knowledge according to the curriculum and stressing educational values – which my mother saw as the mission of her life – she devoted great effort in two other directions, which at that time were considered innovations: the first was preparing her pupils for social and educational integration into Israel, and the second, helping them gain a better understanding of the concept Diaspora and of the Holocaust and the lessons to be learned from it, at a time when the Israeli educational system was barely conscious of those ideas. And, as she had done in the Diaspora, educating her pupils in the spirit of the Zionist vision and its fulfilment in Eretz Israel, so she did in Israel, seeing that her pupils, among other things, acquire a better grasp of the Jewish communities in the Diaspora as well as of the Holocaust that befell our people and the courageous acts performed during those horrifying years.

She had wonderful relations with the other members of

the teaching staff and with the school's principal, Arye Reinish, and vice-principal, Shmuel Guberman. This was noticeable not only at social gatherings but also in their joint clarification of educational problems that came up in the school, searching for fitting solutions, again by appropriate pedagogical means. Long hours on their own time were devoted to this, seeing it as a natural extension of their jobs.

Whenever I returned form my diplomatic service abroad, I saw it as my pleasant duty to visit them at the school to tell them my impressions of what I had seen and heard, particularly about what was going on in the field of education in the Diaspora. We all agreed that without national Jewish education there, the resources for *aliyah* would become poorer and poorer, weakening national attachment to the Jewish people and its state, as a whole.

After retiring from teaching, my mother moved to Jerusalem to live in our vicinity. There, too, she cultivated in her modest apartment an open house – as she had done in Tel Aviv – for her family, old friends with whom she maintained contact, and new friends she made in Jerusalem.

On Tet Vav be-Tevet Tashmah (10 January 1985) she passed away after a long illness and a difficult battle for her life. It was a great loss for all of us. To me, personally, she was an exemplary mother, father, and sister, in the years of hardship and rebirth. We found consolation in the fact that she had lived to see the defeat of Nazism, the rise of the independent Jewish state – Israel – and the fruits of her contribution to the Hebrew educational and teaching system.

In her memory we founded a memorial fund that assisted, among other things, with the publication of Hebrew books and studies on Transnistria, such as *Across the River* by Hanna Meller, *The Burning Ice* by Avigdor Shachan (that appeared also in English), *In Distress* – songs from ghettos and camps, songs of revolt – edited by Ernst Hurvitz, Gil Aldema, and Shlomo Even Shoshan, and *Jewish Children in Transnistria During the Holocaust* by Shmuel Ben-Zion.

*

The day after Israel's proclamation of Independence I started working at Papyrus, a factory manufacturing paper goods, in south Tel Aviv. Next I was employed at the Central Trade Union of Physicians and Nurses of the Histadrut (General Federation of Workers). At the same time I took night courses at a high school for working students, whose director was the teacher Saritzky, on Ferdinand Lasalle Street in Tel Aviv. I finished my workday at 4:00 pm, and by 6:00 pm I was seated behind my school desk. Combining work and studies was difficult, so I stopped taking courses at night after I finished eleventh grade and began to prepare myself for matriculation on my own – no easy feat under our circumstances. It took me two years (instead of one) to complete all exams. By the time I had my matriculation I was 22 years old. I served in the Israel Defence Forces for a short period. During that time I met my wife, Hanna, who was also then a soldier. Afterwards, I spent most of my reserve army duty as a liaison officer to the UN corps in Sinai and the Golan. When I was accepted as a student at the Hebrew University of Jerusalem in the Faculties of Hebrew Literature and History of the Jewish people, I moved, naturally, to Jerusalem. For my livelihood I worked as a secretary at a girls school (No. 3) in Jerusalem and as a substitute teacher at that school. At a later stage, I was accepted at the Ministry of Foreign Affairs. Once I completed my BA degree, I was sent on my first diplomatic mission to Australia, at the end of 1955, as chancellor of Israel's legation in Sydney. I completed my last diplomatic post at the end of 1995 as Israel's ambassador to Austria and the UN Organisations in Vienna as well as non-resident ambassador (seated in Vienna) to Slovakia and Slovenia. In the course of my diplomatic service I earned my MA and PhD degrees, also at the Hebrew University of Jerusalem, in History of the Jewish People and International Relations.

As a Holocaust survivor I have always felt indebted to the State of Israel for granting me the opportunity and great privilege of being part of its diplomatic service for 42 years, representing the country in different capitals of the world and carrying out diverse functions, both abroad and in the Foreign Ministry's headquarters in Jerusalem. There could not have been for me any greater compensation for all those years of hardship in the shadow of destruction.

12. My mother Zadcanit and myself, Tel Aviv, 1952

Epilogue

On 11 September 1985, forty years after the victory over Nazi Germany, the Protocol Head at Romania's Ministry of Foreign Affairs accompanied me in his official car on the way to the Presidential Palace in Bucharest to the ceremony of the presentation of my Credential Letters to President Nicolae Ceausescu as Israel's new Ambassador to the Socialist Republic of Romania.

Romania in those years was the only country in the communist bloc to maintain diplomatic relations with Israel, since all her neighbours in the bloc, including Yugoslavia, had broken off relations with Israel in June 1967 as a result of the Six-Day War.

On the way to the Presidential Palace I could not help thinking of that young boy who was persecuted by those brutal Romanian soldiers, acting on behalf of Romania's fascist government during the war years, and who happened to survive their atrocities only by miracle. That same child was now about to be received by Romania's president as the Special and Plenipotentiary Ambassador of an independent Jewish state. A state established with supreme bravery by sons and daughters of the Jewish people whom the fascist dictator of Romanian had wanted to annihilate – before Hitler and his associates planned the 'final solution of the Jewish people' at the Wannsee Conference – and who even succeeded in part to fulfil his satanic aims, with the murder of tens of thousands of Jews in Bessarabia and Bucovina and the cruel deportation of the massacres' survivors to the ghettos and death camps of Transnistria…

I remembered my mother's untiring efforts and her

rushing around – in Bucharest after the war – to secure a place for me and for her in one of the vessels carrying 'illegal' refugees that sailed from Yugoslavia's shores.

The ceremony for presentation of my Credential Letters was held according to the formal protocol. Romania during its communist era strictly implemented these state procedures. After mutual greetings and my private talk with the President about Israeli–Romanian bilateral relations and the peace process in our region, we exchanged the texts of our speeches for the ceremony. In my text – which had been transmitted to the President two days earlier – I included, among other things, a phrase mentioning 'the Holocaust of the Jews in Europe which did not skip over the Jews in Romania, part of the survivors of which live with us in Israel'. In his text, the President referred to all points I raised in mine, except the reference to the Holocaust in Romania.

During my four-year mission in Romania I held continual discussions with Romanian historians who totally ignored the Holocaust of the Jews in Bessarabia, Bucovina, and Transnistria in their works. I argued with them verbally and in writing; I even presented to universities and research centres valuable documents published in ten volumes on the Holocaust in Romania, edited by Dr Jean Ancel,[48] with the purpose of disseminating knowledge on this subject and making material available to Romanian historians and researchers from reliable sources – including Romanian ones – on the dimension of the Holocaust of the Jews in the territory under Romanian rule in 1941–44. Subsequently, here and there we did notice a reference to this. But Romanian historiography on the whole continued to ignore the subject, even after the anti-communist revolution in Romania at the end of 1989.[49]

Only in April 1997 did the president of Romania, Emil Constantinescu, send an official letter to the president of the Federation of Jewish Communities in Romania, Professor Nicolae Cajal, on the occasion of Holocaust Remembrance Day, admitting – for the first time by a Romanian president – that the

Romanian nation feels itself responsible for the huge tragedy that befell the Jews of Romania during the country's fascist rule … and that the death of hundreds of thousands of Jews on Romanian soil would not be forgotten nor forgiven …

During the course of my mission I, together with my wife, visited Czernowitz. I was the first Israeli ambassador privileged to receive a entry visa, for one day, into Soviet territory in the time of severed diplomatic relations between Israel and the Soviet Union. We crossed the Soviet–Romanian border exactly at the crossing point through which my mother and I had passed in the opposite direction 40 years earlier on our way to Eretz Israel. We were driving the Embassy's car, carrying our national flag. After half an hour's drive we found ourselves on the main street, where we had lived with our family in Czernowitz. This was the same street through which the Red Army soldiers had marched – with me following in their footsteps with great difficulty – to mark Victory Day over Nazi Germany. I had no other aim for the visit now other than a long-time compulsion to march again in this street in Czernowitz, with head held high and with sure steps, marking Victory Day over Nazi Germany, in a distant time and in a different status.

The street had not changed. All its buildings – including the three-story building where we lived before and after the war as well as the structure that had housed the Yiddish state school where I studied in seventh grade – were still standing as a personal monument to all that had been in this town and was no more. The population had changed unrecognisably. Ukrainian and Russian were heard everywhere, not a word in Yiddish or German (two languages widely spoken in Czernowitz before the war). The street was very crowded and noisy. Life seemed to be as hectic as in the bygone days, far, far away from the Holocaust memories.

In Jerusalem at the beginning of 1991 I mentioned to the Chief Rabbi of Romanian Jewry, Dr Moses Rosen, the deep impression made on me by the memorial statue in the courtyard of the Great Synagogue in Budapest, in memory of the

Hungarian Jews who had died in the Holocaust. I suggested to him to erect a similar memorial statue in the courtyard of Bucharest's central synagogue, 'Coral', to commemorate the Jewish Holocaust victims of Bessarabia, Bucovina, and Transnistria on the marking of 50 years to the mass murders of Jews committed by Romanian soldiers in those areas, before the deportation of the surviving Jews to the ghettos and death camps of Transnistria. Chief Rabbi Rosen, an extraordinary personality who accomplished a great deal under the communist regime in Romania – in very difficult circumstances – to preserve the Jewish community, instantly responded favourably, saying he would immediately act towards implementing this idea. And, indeed, by July 1991 the statue had been raised in the Coral synagogue courtyard, in memory of the Jewish victims of the pogroms of Bucharest (1941), Iasi (1941), and the victims in Bessarabia, Bucovina, and Transnistria as well as the Jews of North Transylvania (1944, then under Hungarian rule, deported to the death camp Auschwitz).

Among those attending the unveiling ceremony of this statue were representatives of the Romanian authorities; Israel's Ambassador to Romania, Zvi Mazel; the head of Nativ (Liaison Office, dealing with *aliyah* from Eastern Europe); Judge David Bartov; representatives of Romania's Holocaust survivors living in Israel and elsewhere; representatives of world Jewish organizations; and myself, in the capacity of Deputy Director General for Soviet and East European Affairs in Israel's Ministry of Foreign Affairs, who was invited to unveil the memorial plaque commemorating the Jewish victims in Bessarabia.

Chief Rabbi Rosen delivered a very moving speech as did a number of Holocaust survivors. This is the only memorial statue erected in Romania in memory of Holocaust victims of Bessarabia, Bucovina, and Transnistria in the years 1941–44. A few, scattered statues had been raised in Transnistria under the Soviet regime, simply bearing the inscription 'In memory of Nazi victims', without mentioning – in the Soviet tradition – their Jewish identity.

So far I have refrained from visiting Moghilev. I thought, and I still think, that I would not have the spiritual wherewithal to travel, comfortably, in a car along the road where tens of thousands of Jews from Bessarabia and Bucovina were cruelly treated and forcefully marched to the ghettos and death camps of Transnistria. Hundreds of thousands of them perished during the death march because of exhaustion. Their corpses were slung to the sides of the road as prey for the local farmers who took the victims' clothing and the meagre property they had carried with them as their strength drained away.

I think I would not have been able to walk once again in the streets of the Moghilev ghetto, where each house I had known would have roused unforgettable pictures from my memory: the collection of the corpses in the early morning hours of winter 1941–42 and for many months afterwards, their being loaded onto wagons to take them to mass graves – victims of typhus, hunger, freezing, and suffering. Or, the scene of dozens of orphans wandering through the ghetto streets, skeletons, abandoned, wounded, and rotting, asking for a piece of bread and a bit of mercy.

Some of the Transnistria Holocaust survivors visited Moghilev in June 1998, amongst them my friend, the writer Aaron Apelfeld, together with a team from Israel's Educational Television, to produce a documentary film on the Holocaust of the Jews in Bessarabia, Bucovina, and Transnistria. They were accompanied by the lawyer Itzchak Artzi, an emissary of the Zionist Organization who had visited the Moghilev ghetto in early 1944 in an effort to take Jewish orphans out of Transnistria and transfer them to Jewish communities in Romania. When the visitors returned to Israel they told us that the place is unrecognisable. It has changed completely in the 50 years since the liberation. However, at the entrance to the former ghetto is a memorial plaque, put up by the small Moghilev Jewish community, noting the existence of the ghetto in 1942–44.

They said that the streets of Moghilev are crowded. The

period after Nazi occupation was a beneficial one for the town. It is good to know that life goes on as usual, far from the days of Nazi rule. Some of the small, poor houses have disappeared, making way for new, tall buildings. Along the ways leading from Moghilev eastwards and southwards – the via dolorosa of the deportees – are green, cultivated fields, tranquil and flourishing surroundings, remote from the events that occurred during the Holocaust.[50]

The memory of Transnistria will always be engraved in the minds and hearts of its survivors. Once they are gone, only their testimonies will remain, oral and written, along with the memoirs and studies that have been published, and perhaps may yet still be produced on the basis of documentation known and hitherto undiscovered, and the memorial inscriptions on mass graves scattered throughout Transnistria, Bessarabia, Bucovina, Bucharest, Dorohoi, and Iasi. Another memorial here, another monument there, those standing and those yet to be raised, are testimonials in commemoration of the Holocaust victims who perished in those places. But no memorial can ever express or reflect what happened here or anywhere else in the Holocaust world, the terrible suffering the victims endured on their final journey to their eternal resting places. There may be hundreds, or even thousands, of pits that swallowed up the unknown dead and the murder victims, the earth covering them in unmarked silence, with no sign and no memorial plaque, as if these people had never been…

13. Closing a circle: presenting my letters of credential as Israel's ambassador to Romania to the president of Romania, Nicolai Ceausescu, Bucharest, 1985

14. A ceremony in the courtyard of Bucharest's Coral Synagogue, Bucharest, 1991: as Deputy Director General of the Israel Ministry of Foreign Affairs, I am unveiling a memorial plaque commemorating the Jews of Bessarabia who perished during the Holocaust

15. The front courtyard of the Coral Synagogue, Bucharest, 1991: the statue of remembrance in memory of the Jews of Bessarabia, Bucovina, Transylvania, Transnistria, Bucharest, Dorohoi, and Iasi who perished in the Holocaust

16. Memorial to the Holocaust victims of Transnistria, Hall of Remembrance, Yad Vashem, Jerusalem

Notes

1. Although in the secret Protocol attached to the Non-Aggression Pact between the Soviet Union and Nazi Germany only Bessarabia was mentioned as an area to be 'under Soviet influence', the Soviet government demanded in its ultimatum to Romania that North Bucovina should also be transferred to its sphere of influence as compensation for Romania's holding Bessarabia – a territory the Soviet Union saw as its own – under its rule from 1918. In fact, talks about to whom it belonged were held between the Soviet Union and Romania from the time it was annexed to the latter in 1918. Before submitting its ultimatum to Romania, the Soviet Union had wanted to annex the entire area of Bucovina, but since Germany did not approve of this, the Soviet Union agreed in negotiations with Germany to relinquish its demand for South Bucovina. Romania was unaware of this secret understanding between Germany and the Soviet Union, so it asked Germany for advice concerning the Soviet ultimatum given to Romania to retreat from Bessarabia and North Bucovina within 48 hours. Germany, of course, told Romania to agree to the demand. Since the expected support from Germany was not forthcoming, Romania was compelled to retreat from the designated areas within the time allotted without a fight. The suggestion to oppose the Soviet Union by force was actually raised at the meeting of the 'Crown Council'. It was, however, rejected by a majority of votes since the council members felt Romania had no chance of winning a war against the Soviet Union.
2. The mass murders have been documented as follows:
   Marius Mircu, *Pogromurile din Bessarabia şi Bucovina* (in Romanian) [The Pogroms in Bessarabia and Bucovina] (Bucharest: Globe, 1947);
   M. Carp, *Transnistriă* (in Yiddish) (Buenos Aires: Union of Jews from Bessarabia in Argentina, 1950) – the book contains a summary based on Carp's three volumes called *Cartea Neagra* (in Romanian) [Black Book] (Bucharest: 1947);
   The collection of documents edited by Jean Ancel in 12 volumes: *Documents Concerning the Fate of Romanian Jewry During the Holocaust* (New York: Beate Klarsfeld Foundation, 1985);
   Jean Ancel, *Romania: History of the Holocaust*, 2 vols. (in Hebrew) (Jerusalem: Yad Vashem, 2002);
   Jean Ancel, *Transnistria 1941–1942*, 3 vols., History and Document Summary, The Romanian Mass Murder Campaigns (Tel Aviv: Tel Aviv University, 2003);
   Pinkas ha-Kehillot, Romania (in Hebrew), vol.1, pp.349–88 (Transnistria), vol.1, pp.461–73 (Moghilev) (Jerusalem: Yad Vashem, 1970).
3. David Schaary, historian of Bucovina Jewry, briefed me – at my request – on some important data on the history of the Seminar for Hebrew Kindergarten Teachers and on the Hebrew Teachers College, both in Czernowitz. He told me the following:

   The Seminar for Hebrew Kindergarten Teachers (Pedagogion) of Czernowitz. With the transfer of Bucovina from Austrian rule to that of Romania, the Jewish public began to act towards the setting up of a Hebrew net of Jewish education. The *Safa Ivriya* (Hebrew Language) Association, founded in Czernowitz in 1905, had taken the initiative on this in 1920 with the establishment of a seminar to train Hebrew kindergarten teachers to work in the Hebrew kindergartens that opened in that period throughout Bucovina. The Seminar also organized advanced studies for Hebrew teachers who gave private or public Hebrew lessons ... The first class finished a six-month program but as time went on the course of study was expanded to two years. The first director of the 'Pedagogion' was Dr Herman Sternberg, followed by Dr Ephraim Porat. In 1924, ten students were registered in the Seminar of Kindergarten Teachers; in 1925, fourteen; in 1927, eighteen; and in 1929, fifty. Many students from Bessarabia attended the advanced studies courses for private Hebrew teachers. Numerous young teachers from Bessarabia served as private Hebrew teachers in Jewish homes in Bucovina.

Hebrew Teachers College. In October 1926, around the time Rabbi Abraham Mark was elected chief rabbi of Czernowitz, a modest college opened for training teachers of Hebrew subjects under the direction of Dr Bendit Gottlieb. It offered a two-year course of studies. This was almost the only institution in Romania for training teachers in Hebrew subjects (a short-term course functioned for a short time in Iasi in 1921). Even in Bessarabia, where a wide network of Hebrew schools operated, including kindergartens, elementary and secondary schools under the guidance of the *Tarbut* Association, the Romanian authorities did not permit the operation of any institution for training Hebrew teachers. The Hebrew Teachers College in Czernowitz received limited public financial support, and the students had to live in dormitories under the most illogical conditions. In 1927 twenty-two students were enrolled in the college (in the two-year program). In 1929 there were about twenty-four. Over time the number of students declined, and in 1935 only fifteen were studying there.

4. My late uncle Yosef Lerner: Czernowitz–Dorna–Bucharest–Haifa; my late aunt Atara Lerner-Kulinsky, Czernowitz–Chile–Peru–Colombia–Tel Aviv; my late mother, Zadcanit (Fradia) Lerner-Hurvitz, Czernowitz–Berhomet–Falticeni–Oradea–Dorna–Edinitz–Bucharest–Cyprus–Tel Aviv; my late aunt Sonia Lerner–Barles, Czernowitz–Iacobeni–Haifa; my aunt Nechama (Netty) Lerner, Falticeni–Czernowitz–Colombia; my late aunt Batia Lerner–Sinnreich, Czernowitz; my aunt Shoshana (Rosa) Lerner–Bromberg, Czernowitz–Bucharest–Cyprus–Haifa.
5. My late mother, Zadcanit Hurvitz, published an article, 'My Parents' Home in Zabriceni' (in Hebrew), in *Yad le-Edinitz* (Tel Aviv: Association of Jews from Edinitz, 1973), pp.463–4.
6. According to the testimony given by a Transnistria survivor, Dora Rosenberg-Lencovsky, US resident.
7. *Pinkas ha-Kehillot, Romania* (Jerusalem: Yad Vashem, 1980), vol.2, p.324, lists 5,341 Jews in Edinitz according to the 1930 census, then constituting 90 per cent of the local population. The number I am citing is based on the estimate quoted for Edinitz under Soviet rule 1940–41. One should also take into account the increase by birth among the Jewish population for the years 1930–41, as well as the immigration of Jews to Edinitz from the surrounding villages and from elsewhere in Romania during that year of Soviet rule.
8. My aunt (my mother's sister) Sonia Lerner was a graduate of the Hebrew Teachers College in Czernowitz. Before her *aliyah* to Eretz Israel in 1935, she worked as a teacher in the Bucovina town of Iacobeni. She belonged to the Gordonia movement and within its framework did her *hachshara* (training) towards her move to Eretz Israel. She was a member of kibbutz Yagur for about ten years. Upon her marriage to Zeev Rubinstein Barles, she left the kibbutz and settled in Haifa. They have both passed away. Their daughter Zipora Barles-Fink

is a graduate of a teachers and kindergarten teachers training college in Haifa and works in the field of education in Haifa.

9. Liova Gukovsky (later Yehuda Achisar) was active in the *Po'alei Zion* movement in Edinitz. Several years after joining kibbutz Yagur, he left on a mission to Romania on behalf of the Dror movement (1937–40). He was the first parachutist from Eretz Israel to parachute behind enemy lines, into Romania (1943). He was captured immediately and put in jail. After his release from prison in 1944 he returned to the kibbutz. In 1947 he left for a mission in the refugee camps on Cyprus. He lost his life in 1954 in an air accident at kibbutz Maagan. His autobiographical work, *To What I Was Called* (in Hebrew) appeared in Tel Aviv in 1953.
10. A member of kibbutz Hanita, Yasha (Jacob) Navon (Hahamovici) gave me the names of dozens of Edinitz *halutzim* (pioneers) who, within the Gordonia movement's activities, joined new settlements – Massada, Avuka, Hulda, Nir Am and Hanita – in the 1930s.
11. His daughter Frieda Kuzminer-Mei Tal, a retired teacher in Tel Aviv, was also my teacher when I studied at her late father's elementary school. She was in Edinitz when the mass murder took place and was deported afterwards to Transnistria. About her father she recalled that during the days of the massacre, her father – my teacher – organized a group of men from among local Jews to defend their families and the honour of forty women hidden in a cellar for fear of being raped. Only because of their resistance did they succeed in preventing the Romanian soldiers from breaking into the cellar to attack the women. Yet all of these defenders were murdered. See *Yad le-Edinitz*, p.733.
12. My uncle (my father's brother), the late Meir Gurvitz, owned a shop in the village of his birth, Badragi. With the annexation of Bessarabia to the Soviet Union, he moved with his wife Feiga and his two daughters to Edinitz, from where all four were deported to Siberia. On the way, my uncle was separated from his family, never to meet them again. My uncle and aunt perished in Siberia. After the war, the two sisters, Sara and Ethel, managed to escape under false identities to Kolomia, Ukraine. Sara perished in a tragic accident, in Edinitz; Ethel emigrated to Israel and passed away in Jerusalem in 1973.
13. Quoted from Alexander Wert's book, *Russia during the War, 1941–1945* (in Hebrew) (Tel Aviv: Maarakhot, 1968), vol.1, pp.107–8, quoted from the Russian source 'The Great Patriotic War of the Soviet Union', vol. 1, pp.434–5.
14. Estimates of murdered Jews are based on information that spread among the Jewish residents of Edinitz after the massacre. This number also appears in *Pinkas ha-Kehillot: Romania*, vol. 2, Edinitz, p.325.
15. See note 10.
16. Ita (my father's sister) and her husband Haim perished in the Holocaust; their son Buma (Avraham) Grinberg survived and is now with us in Israel; Kreine Bronfman (my father's sister) was saved after finding refuge in a Ukranian village in Transnistria, where she worked as a seamstress, hiding her Jewish identity; Lea (my father's sister) perished in Transnistria and her daughter Dora Groisman-Razlog, who was saved, is now with us in Israel – both of them came from the Cucunesti village in Bessarabia, near the Prut River; my cousins Buma and Dora were saved thanks to my aunt Kreine who collected them and kept them with her in the Ukrainian village; Fradia (my father's sister), her husband Berl, and their son Yosipil Fein, from the village of Badragi, Bessarabia, perished in the Holocaust.
17. Detailed description in the testimony in *Yad le-Edinitz*, pp.729–42.
18. Carp, *Transnistria*, p.29.
19. Ibid., pp.115–16.
20. Ibid., pp.116–17.
21. I referred to it in my book, *The Jewish Factor in the Relations Between Nazi Germany*

and the Soviet Union (in Hebrew) (Jerusalem: Magnes Press of the Hebrew University, 1986).

22. Details about the murdered Jewish personalities: *Pinkas ha-Kehillot: Romania*, vol.2, pp.504–5.
23. According to the 1930 census, 45,592 Jews resided in Czernowitz, constituting 40.5 per cent of its total population. The number of Jewish residents I mention is based on the information spread amongst the Jewish residents themselves, before the deportation to Transnistria. In this case, as in the case of Edinitz, one should take into account the natural growth of the Jewish population in town between 1930 and 1941 as well as the migration of Jews to Czernowitz from Austria and Czechoslovakia after their annexation to Germany, the many Jews who ran away from Poland to Czernowitz after the outbreak of the Second World War, and the migration of Jews from Romania to Czernowitz when North Bucovina was annexed to the Soviet Union. The number of 70,000 Jews living in Czernowitz before the German-Romanian invasion was also mentioned by the mayor of Czernowitz in 1941–42, Traian Popovici, in the 'confession' he left after the war. Carp, *Transnistria*, p.191.
24. According to the census of the Romanian authorities after they occupied Czernowitz and before the deportation of Jews to Transnistria, Carp *Transnistria*, p.193; and *Pinkas ha-Kehillot: Romania*, vol.2, p.507.
25. My late uncle Yosef Lerner was the personal secretary of our great poet H.N. Bialik, during his studies in Odessa before the October Revolution of 1917. A versatile scholar, in his youth he was greatly involved in pedagogical activity and, later on, in trade. He left for South America (Brazil and Peru); he returned from there and settled in Czernowitz at the beginning of the 1930s. With his wife, the late Hanna née Kogan (died in Haifa in 1986), they both cultivated a warm home that served as a hostel for all the members of the family. In 1947 they embarked for Eretz Israel, with their son Jacob, aboard the *Geula*, a ship that carried illegal immigrants; they were exiled to the refugee camps of Cyprus and released after Israel became independent and settled in Haifa, where my uncle worked at Haifa's Port Authority as well as in education. He died in his home at the age of 102 in 1997. His son Dr Jacob Lerner is a psychiatrist and until recently was director of the Eytanim (psychiatric) hospital in Jerusalem.
26. My late grandmother, Lea Lerner, emigrated to Israel together with her son, Yosef, her daughter-in-law Hanna, her grandson Jacob, and her daughter Shoshana Lerner (who was together with us in Transnistria). She lived with her daughter Shoshana and her son-in-law, Haim Bromberg, in Haifa, where she died in 1953.
27. Traian Popovici published an article on this story: 'Mein Kenntnis' [My Confession, translated into German from Romanian], in *The History of the Jews in Bucovina* (in German), ed. Gold (Tel Aviv: Olamenu, 1962), vol.2, p.62. He writes there, *inter alia*, that 'The deportation to Transnistria was regarded as an unwise act by Marshal Antonescu – an inhuman, barbarous, and wild act that deeply shattered the existence of our people (Romanian), an act that released the dark instincts of human hatred'.
28. My late aunt Batia, graduate of the Teachers College in Czernowitz in the 1930s, taught Hebrew in Czernowitz until the town was annexed by the Soviet Union. Her husband, Jacob Sinnreich, who was recruited into the Red Army shortly before the German-Romanian occupation of Czernowitz, never returned. She immigrated to Israel in 1958 where she remarried; her second husband, Moshe Peri, was one of the veteran settlers in Rehovoth. Both of them cultivated a warm home. They are no longer living. Their daughter Gila Preiss lives with her husband and three sons in Rehovoth.
29. My aunt Shoshana, a graduate of the Teachers College in Czernowitz in the 1930s,

engaged in Hebrew teaching in Bucovina until its annexation by the Soviet Union. Afterwards she taught in a Moldavian school (under Soviet rule); she was together with us in Czernowitz when Nazi Germany and fascist Romania invaded the Soviet Union. She emigrated to Israel in 1948, after a year's exile in the refugee camps of Cyprus, and soon became involved in education as a teacher at the Haia Ziev public school in Haifa. Until her retirement she was a member of the Histadrut Council and of the executive committee of the Teachers Council for the Jewish National Fund in Haifa and taught students of the State Teachers College Gordon in Haifa. She was married to the late Haim Bromberg, a Holocaust survivor. They maintained an open, warm home for all their relatives and friends. Their son, Yehoshua, graduated as an electronic engineer from the Technion, Israel's technological institute in Haifa.

30. Sioma Kunis unfortunately passed away a few years after his arrival in Israel with his family. He worked until his last minute in his profession as a physician at one of Haifa's hospitals.
31. Jacob Kornblitt, an engineer, was deported to Transnistria from Radauti (South Bucovina). He lived in our crowded house in the Moghilev ghetto together with his parents, brother, and two sisters. After liberation, he returned with his family to Radauti and from there, several years later, emigrated to Israel. He worked as an engineer in Haifa until his death in 1995.
32. See his book, *Jagendorf's Foundry* (New York: Harper and Collins, 1991).
33. The late advocate Simcha Sobe, Doctor of Law, resided in Cimpulung, South Bucovina, before his deportation to Transnistria. He completed his studies in Czernowitz. He was a survivor of the Moghilev ghetto. Soon after his migration to Israel he began to work as a lawyer for the Tel Aviv State Attorney. He died of a heart attack in the 1950s when in his thirties. He left no family.
34. *Hatikvah* (The Hope), composed by N.H. Imber, became Israel's national anthem after having been sung from the early twentieth century as the Zionist anthem. *Techezakna* (Be Strong), composed by H.N. Bialik in the late nineteenth century, became an anthem of the Zionist socialist movement.
35. The 'rescue committee' was founded by representatives of the Zionist movements in Romania. The Jews Centre was established by fascist Romanian authorities, after having dissolved the Federation of Jewish Communities of Romania, presided over by Dr W. Filderman. As head of the Jews Centre they nominated Dr N. Gingold, a medical doctor, who was a converted Jew.
36. After the liberation of Romania from its fascist regime (23 August 1944), Dr W. Filderman returned to his previous function as president of the Federation of Jewish Communities in Romania, a position from which he was removed by the fascist authorities in 1941, when they founded the Jews Centre. Dr Filderman carried out this function from 1944 to 1948, when he was compelled to leave Romania secretly, owing to the incitement of the Jewish communists (Jewish Democratic Committee) against him. From then until 1963 he lived in Paris, *inter alia*, working on his memoirs. He visited Israel twice. His personal archive was transferred to Yad Vashem Institute, in Jerusalem, which in 1974 published a list of the subjects from Filderman's archive, under the editorship of Dr Jean Ancel, who also wrote a biographical preface about Filderman's personality, his functions and activities for the sake of Romanian Jewry, before and during the war. Also, Sh. Shaferman published *Dr W. Filderman: 50 Years of Romanian Jewish History* (in Hebrew) (Tel Aviv: 1989). The book surveys Filderman's personality and his activities in the fateful hours of Romanian Jewry.
37. See Dr Shmuel Ben-Zion's book, *Jewish Children in Transnistria during the Holocaust* (in Hebrew) (Haifa: Haifa University and Beit Lohamei Haghetaot, Institute of Holocaust Research, 1989). Chapter three, pp.140–200, deals with orphanages and education institutes in the ghettos.

38. For instance, Dr Efraim Ofir's article, 'Was it possible to rescue 70,000 Jews from Transnistria?' (in Hebrew), *Yalkut Moreshet*, 33 (1982).
39. Sh. Ben-Zion, *Jewish Children in Transnistria*, pp.227–39.
40. See my article, 'Edinitz – after Liberation from Nazi occupation' (in Hebrew), *Edut* (Beit Lohamei Haghetaot, April 1992).
41. Lea Lerner; Yosef, Hanna, and Jacob Lerner; Shoshana Lerner; my mother Zadcanit Hurvitz and me.
42. Shaike Dan's activities were described in Amos Ettinger's book, *Blind Jump: The Story of Yeshayahu (Shaike) Dan* (in Hebrew) (Tel Aviv: Zmora, Bitan, 1986).
43. Ibid., pp.191–2.
44. Abba Berditchev was born in Romania, where he was an activist in the Zionist movement. He emigrated to Israel in 1941. He was one of the Eretz Israel parachutists who jumped behind enemy lines. He was caught in Slovakia by the Germans and executed in the extermination camp at Mauthausen, Austria, in early 1945. During my mission as Israel's Ambassador to Austria (1993–95) we placed a memorial plaque at the (presumed) place of his execution.
45. For instance the titles that were followed by editorials: 'Knesset Israel' [meaning the Yishuv] demands letting the refugees of the *Knesset Israel* into the country', *Davar*, 26 Nov. 1946; 'By force and by bloodshed were the refugees expelled on the destroyers', 27 Nov. 1946; 'A voice of anger rings in the Yishuv', 28 Nov. 1946. 'Let the 4,000 refugees not be expelled from the homeland', *Haaretz*, 26 Nov. 1946; a photo of the *Knesset Israel* ship appeared alongside relevant articles on the refugees' fighting their being expelled, 27 Nov. 1946; 'The refugees will not be expelled before a decision is handed down', 28 Nov. 1946.
    Itschak Artzi, one of the *Knesset Israel* refugees and one of its leaders, published a travel diary that covered the happenings from the day the ship sailed from the Yugoslav shore until its arrival at Haifa port. See *Masua*, an annual collection of articles on the history of the Holocaust (April 1979), as well as his article on the expulsion to Cyprus, based on his memoirs in *Masua* (April 1984).
46. *Davar*, 26 Nov. 1946 and 1 Dec. 1946.
47. Central Zionist Archive, File 25/2600S.
48. See note 2c.
49. Y. Govrin, 'Transnistria and the Holocaust in Romanian Historiography', *Jews in Eastern Europe*, 3/43 (Centre for Research and Documentation of East European Jewry, Hebrew University of Jerusalem, Winter 2000).
50. For instance, Nava Semel's article in *Maariv, Musaf Sukkot*, 4 Oct. 1998.

The Library of Holocaust Testimonies

Scorched

Irit Amiel

Translated from the Hebrew by Riva Rubin

The heroes of the stories in this book are people who in the hell of the Holocaust were doomed for life, people who speak only with reluctance about their past, about the heavy baggage of their life's experiences. Being a witness, Irit Amiel uses the memories of her childhood friends and translates the long silences of people living in the Israeli melting pot into testimony. The stories are written in a simple and restrained way, but the voices coming out touch the most profound human feelings. Each story is powerful and often painful, but is imbued with a sense of hope.

> 'There is immediacy and a strength to each of these stories that makes it clear just how much they derive from real experience. The emphasis is on individuals, and on their characters. Each person whose story Irit Amiel tells lives again in these pages.'
>
> From the Foreword by Sir Martin Gilbert

September 2006, 94 pages
ISBN 978 0 85303 634 0

The Library of Holocaust Testimonies

Hiding in the Open:
A Young Fugitive in Nazi-Occupied Poland
Zenon Neumark

This is the story of Zenon Neumark's experiences as a Jewish teenager in Nazi-occupied Europe. He escaped from a forced labour camp in Tomaszow Mazowiecki, Poland, and lived under a false Polish Catholic identity, first in Warsaw and later in Vienna. It is a story about betrayal by friends and rescue by strangers; about a constant fear of being recognized as a Jew; the struggle for lodgings, work and blending in with the local population; a story of a double life working for opposing Resistance groups and opportunities to help others survive. The story ends with his recapture in the Warsaw Uprising of 1944 and deportation to a camp in Vienna, where, after another escape, he was liberated by the Soviet Army.

September 2006, 216 pages
ISBN 978 0 85303 633 3

The Library of Holocaust Testimonies

My Own Vineyard: A Jewish Family in Krakow Between the Wars

Miriam Akavia

This rich novel, in the best tradition of family sagas, tells the story of three generations of a Jewish family in Krakow, from the beginning of the twentieth century to the eve of the German occupation of Poland in September 1939. The story of this large, middle-class Jewish family is also the story of a deeply-rooted Jewish community and its considerable cultural and material achievements, until disaster strikes and it is wiped off the face of the earth.

At the beginning of the century, Krakow was under Austrian rule. The mother of the family died, leaving a husband and eight children. A different destiny awaited each of the children, each story reflecting the options which faced Polish Jews at that time. With the outbreak of the First World War, the eldest son joined the army and was sent to the Italian front. He returned a broken man, and died shortly afterwards. The second son married happily, became a successful lumber merchant and a paterfamilias. He veered between Jewish and European culture and regarded Poland as his homeland. One of the sisters, a natural rebel, fell in love with a Polish non-Jew. When he abandoned her, she became a Zionist and emigrated to Eretz Israel. Her older sister was happily married to an old-style religious Jew. Another sister married an assimilated Jew and was uncertain as to her national identity, while the fourth fell in love with a communist. Their prosperous brother had three children – two daughters and a son – who enjoyed life in independent Poland between the wars. When the Germans invaded Poland, the family missed the last train out and with it the chance to be saved. Most of the family perished in the Holocaust.

September 2006, 340 pages
ISBN 978 0 85303 519 0

The Library of Holocaust Testimonies

The Girl in the Check Coat
Survival in Wartime Poland and a New Life in Australia

Christine Winecki

Translated from the Hebrew by Chris Samplawski

Christine Winecki is a Holocaust child survivor. In her book she presents the story of her life, starting with the fond memories of her early childhood in south-eastern Poland, and then taking the reader through the turbulent years of the Second World War under Soviet and then German occupation. She depicts also the story of her future husband Oton – a survivor of a labour camp in Siberia – and their post-war life in Warsaw until the infamous events in 1968, which forced them to leave Poland and emigrate to Australia.

Apart from its biographical content the book is rich in observations on the historical, political and ethnographic aspects of the changing settings of the author's unfolding story. Her first book, *From Stanislawow to Australia* (in Polish), was published in 1999. Christine Winecki and her husband Oton live in Melbourne. They have two daughters and five grandchildren.

November 2006, 240 pages
ISBN 978 0 85303 657 7

The Library of Holocaust Testimonies

In Hiding
Surviving an Abusive 'Protector' and the Nazi Occupation of Holland

Benno Benninga with William Halstead

When the German army invades the Netherlands in 1940, the Jewish family of Jacques and Reina Benninga, their teenage son Benno and daughter Mia attempt escape to England, but fail. They then try to comply with the Nazis' increasingly stringent anti-Jewish edicts until submission is intolerable and potentially life-threatening. Assuming the war would soon end, a Dutch couple agrees to hide the Benninga family for a large fee. As the Second World War and the Nazi occupation stretches on, their hostess becomes mentally and physically abusive. The couple's wartime business venture itself has the potential for disaster – she and her husband are active black marketeers, and a local police officer lives just across the road. Through it all, Jacques Benninga keeps a daily journal – a remarkable document which the authors have found an invaluable source to amplify Benno's gripping eyewitness memories of the family's nerve-wracking, life-threatening, two years in hiding.

November 2006, 188 pages
ISBN 978 0 85303 632 6

The Library of Holocaust Testimonies

The Single Light
From Boyhood to Manhood and from Nazism and Communism to Freedom
Ernest Levy
Compiled and Adapted by David Spear

Ernest Levy, the youngest of eight, was born into a strong Orthodox family, and achieved his Bar Mitzvah as Nazism reached into Czechoslovakia and expelled Jews of Hungarian origin back across the border. From there his story takes us through the war years, via Auschwitz, to the labour camps, from where, as the Russians closed in, inmates were force-marched to Belsen. Ernest survived Belsen and typhoid to choose repatriation. Finding himself back in Budapest, a crisis of faith, brought on by the hideous experiences of his teens, led him to flirt with communism, but reviving faith and a passion for music won the day and established his future. Since finding a home in Scotland in the early 1960s, he has committed himself to educating and enlightening the young people around him of events which otherwise would only appear in a history book.

January 2007, 358 pages
ISBNs 978 0 85303 747 7 and 748 4

The Library of Holocaust Testimonies

Recollections and Reflections How I Turned Despair into an Appreciation of Life

Jack Brauns

This memoir contains many fascinating vignettes about pre-war childhood in the Lithuanian city of Kaunas, a child's-eye-view of the lost world of East European Jewry. It also tells the tormented story of the Kovno ghetto as seen by a youngster whose father was a leading figure in the medical life of the ghetto. The author then recounts the long, harsh journey of entering the gates of Dante's *Inferno* into the whirlpool of the Holocaust – to Stutthof and Dachau – and moves on to describe his liberation. The author also provides a full and fascinating focus on the post-war years: recovery, organizing education in Italy, and the struggles of starting a new life in the United States, including the high point of obtaining the release of the author's parents from the Soviet Union at the height of the Cold War.

Jack Brauns has written a most personal and engaging tale; not only is it a powerful factual narrative, but it is also an uplifting one that rises above the cruelties and savageries of the Holocaust, and is full of hope. During his lifetime many people came into his life and like the wind some caressed him gently and some left him bruised. However, they influenced his thinking, behavior and personality, and shaped his life.

It deserves to be widely read, not least among young people, for whom it is a clarion call to emulate the best instincts of humanity.

February 2007, 280 pages
ISBN 978 0 85303 749 1

The Library of Holocaust Testimonies

Sentenced to Life
The Story of a Survivor of the Lahwah Ghetto
Kopel Kolpanitzky
Translated from the Hebrew by Zvi Shulman

Kopel Kolpanitzky grew up in Lahwah, Byelorussia. His entire family was murdered in the Lahwah ghetto uprising against the Nazis, except for his father, who had previously been imprisoned by the Soviets. Living in the forests, he joined a partisan unit and then fought as a soldier in the Red Army. After the war he left the army and in trying to reach Eretz Yisrael almost reached the shores of Palestine before the ship he was on was stopped by the British and its passengers sent to a camp in Cyprus. A year later he finally arrived in Eretz Yisrael just before Israel's independence. He served in the Israel Defence Forces and later entered into business with his father, who had joined him in Israel in the early 1950s.

March 2007, 288 pages
ISBN 978 0 85303 695 1

9780853036432